Problem Solving and Reasoning Skills for PEP Maths: NSC Edition

The publishers would like to thank Rising Stars for their kind permission to reproduce the following copyright material:

Trevor Dixon and Sarah-Anne Fernandes – 9781471880186

Caroline Clissold, Heather Davis, Linda Glithro, Steph King – 9781783395279

Tim Handley and Paul Wrangles – 9781471885129

Tim Handley, Paul Wrangles, Nicki Allman – 9781510403680

Tim Handley – 9781783391783

Hachette UK's policy is to use papers that are natural, renewable and recyclable products and made from wood grown in well-managed forests and other controlled sources. The logging and manufacturing processes are expected to conform to the environmental regulations of the country of origin.

Orders: please contact Hachette UK Distribution, Hely Hutchinson Centre, Milton Road, Didcot, Oxfordshire, OX11 7HH. Telephone: +44 (0)1235 827827. Email education@hachette.co.uk Lines are open from 9 a.m. to 5 p.m., Monday to Friday. You can also order through our website: www.hoddereducation.co.uk

ISBN: 9781510467668

© Paul Broadbent 2019

First published in 2019 by

Hodder Education,

An Hachette UK Company

Carmelite House

50 Victoria Embankment

London EC4Y 0DZ

www.hoddereducation.com

The authorised representative in the EEA is Hachette Ireland, 8 Castlecourt Centre, Dublin 15, D15 XTP3, Ireland (email: info@hbgi.ie)

Impression number   10 9 8 7 6 5 4 3 2

Year   2025

All rights reserved. Apart from any use permitted under UK copyright law, no part of this publication may be reproduced or transmitted in any form or by any means, electronic or mechanical, including photocopying and recording, or held within any information storage and retrieval system, without permission in writing from the publisher or under licence from the Copyright Licensing Agency Limited. Further details of such licences (for reprographic reproduction) may be obtained from the Copyright Licensing Agency Limited, www.cla.co.uk

Cover artwork by Peter Lubach

Illustrations by Peter Lubach and Aptara Ltd.

Typeset in FS Albert 12/14 pts by Aptara Inc.

Printed by CPI Group (UK) Ltd, Croydon CR0 4YY

A catalogue record for this title is available from the British Library.

Contents

How to use this book — 4

1. Number and place value — 5
2. Decimal calculation — 9
3. Formulae and equations — 13
4. Calculation problems — 17
5. Algebra — 21
6. Number problems — 25
7. Multiplication — 29
8. Area and perimeter — 33
9. Three-dimensional shapes — 37
10. Data — 41
11. Mental calculation — 45
12. Multiples, factors and primes — 49
13. Fractions — 53
14. Fractions, decimals, percentages — 57
15. Percentages — 61
16. Ratio and proportion — 65
17. Area of shapes — 69
18. Volume — 73
19. Coordinates and transformations — 77
20. Number sequences — 81
21. Finding all possibilities — 85
22. Exploring shapes — 89
23. Money problems — 93
24. Scaling and ratio — 97
25. Division problems — 101
26. Circles and shapes — 105
27. Angles — 109

How to use this book

Problem Solving and Reasoning Skills for PEP Maths is aligned to Jamaica's National Standards Curriculum. The workbook is designed to systematically develop problem solving and reasoning skills. Learners are encouraged to explore and communicate solutions to everyday scenarios, while teachers/parents are provided with meaningful support to guide learners towards better problem solving and reasoning skills.

First, work through the **Thinking starters** to warm up the problem solving and reasoning skills you already have.

Next, move on to the **Maths mastery** section where you and your classmates can find different solutions to the same situation. It is important to understand that there are many right solutions to problems and many ways of arriving at those solutions.

Afterwards, tackle the **Problem solving** scenario, which tells you the specific reasoning skills that are being developed. Use the prompts in the *Things to think about* box to help you understand the context and find possible solutions. You also get to apply these refreshed skills to an extension activity in the *Your challenge* section. Are your methods and solutions always the same as your classmates'?

Parents/Teachers, **Support notes** on the Maths mastery pages provide practical tips to help you support your learners and the **Tips for success** section provides support for the Problem solving scenario; activity suggestions, extension activities, stimulus questions and a space for your own notes. Answers can be found online at www.hoddereducation.com/PEPMaths

1 Number and place value

Thinking starters

1. Answer these.

   a) Write the value of the 3 in each number.

   932 841   67.913

   b) Write these numbers in order, starting with the smallest.

   3 749 634   3 749 851   3 748 968

   c) Write these numbers in order, starting with the largest.

   5.935   5.9   5.96

   d) Use < or > to make this number statement true.

   5.798   5.98

2. Solve these problems.

   a) Ben has these number cards.

   | 7 | 8 | 2 | 9 | 5 | 6 | 4 |

   What is the largest number below 6 000 000 that Ben can make?

   b) Ali uses three numbers.

   | 5 | 2 | 7 |

   Write two numbers he can make that have 5 thousandths.

3. These 3 numbers are in descending order.

   72456.91   34822.6   96257

   Explain where Errol has gone wrong and why.

Maths mastery

Comparing and rounding large numbers

Jeni and Gavin are playing a computer game.
Jeni has a score of 120 212.
Gavin has a score of 102 678.
Gavin is arguing with Jeni as he thinks he has got the higher score.

- What should Jeni say to Gavin to convince him that she has the higher score?

Jeni's score rounded to the nearest thousand is 120 000.

- What is Gavin's score rounded to the nearest thousand?

Show the method you used to solve the problem. Is it similar to or different from those used by your classmates?

Support notes

Support children with recording their numbers on a place-value grid and Gattegno chart, as shown below for the number 8839, and using this to help identify which number is largest and which digits we need to look at when rounding.

100 000	200 000	300 000	400 000	500 000	600 000	700 000	800 000	900 000
10 000	20 000	30 000	40 000	50 000	60 000	70 000	80 000	90 000
1 000	2 000	3 000	4 000	5 000	6 000	7 000	(8 000)	9 000
100	200	300	400	500	600	700	(800)	900
10	20	(30)	40	50	60	70	80	90
1	2	3	4	5	6	7	8	(9)

Problem solving

Reasoning skills
- Working systematically
- Using numerical reasoning

Number detective

Kevin is playing a computer game. He needs to enter the castle to complete the game. First he must find the secret passcode by answering a set of mystery clues.

- It is a 5-digit integer.
- It is < 20 000.
- The digit in the ten thousands column and the digit in the ones column are the same.
- The digit in the thousands column is prime and odd.
- The digit in the hundreds column is square.
- The digit in the tens column is half the digit in the hundreds column.
- The number rounds to 10 000 when rounded to the nearest 10 000.
- The number is . . .

Things to think about
- What properties of number do you know?
- What do the < and > signs mean?
- If you know what a number rounds to, what does this tell you about the number?
- When you write your own clues, how can you avoid giving away the answer too early?

Your challenge

Can you use your skills as a number detective to help Kevin find the passcode number?

Can you then write your own set of seven clues for a new secret number passcode?

Show the method you used to solve the problem. Is it similar to or different from those used by your classmates?

Tips for success

Use the 'Zooming in' strategy. Say: *Write a number ... a number with four digits ... that is more than 5000 ... that is even ... that is a multiple of 10 ... that is less than 5500 ... where the digit in the tens place is even and square ... where the digit in the hundreds place is 1 less than the tens digit. What is your number?* (5340)

Discuss which numbers children found. When did they have to change their numbers? When were they certain of each digit?

Children identify mystery numbers by following clues that use a range of different number properties and mathematical facts. They create their own similar problems for others to solve. The clues start very broadly and narrow down as children progress through each one. This activity is based on the 'Zooming in' strategy and encourages children to reason about the properties of numbers and their digits.

Children will identify some digits in the numbers earlier than others. Encourage them to record these in their final answer as soon as they feel confident with the digits. Children will use a range of mathematical knowledge and number properties, including prime (numbers with only two factors), square (numbers above 1 with an odd number of factors), multiples and the <, =, > signs. Children may find it difficult to identify the solution to some clues. Encourage them either to isolate the digit (for example, if the clue refers to the tens digit) or consider the whole number (if the digit refers to the whole number).

Using the placeholders alongside each clue will help children identify patterns in the digits and record their answers clearly.

Try this

Support
Children should work in mixed-ability trios. They may benefit from sets of digit cards, which they can physically manipulate to create the numbers using the clues.

Extension
Children should be encouraged to write their own problems with numbers up to 10 000 000 and with up to three decimal places.

Progress notes

Use this space to make your own notes.

2 Decimal calculation

Thinking starters

1 Answer these.

   a) Work out the missing number.

   $0.7 \times 8 = \boxed{} \div 4$

   b) $\boxed{} \times \boxed{} = 2.4$

   What could the missing numbers be? Find two solutions.

   c) $0.6 \times 7 = 4.2$

   Use this fact to solve:

   $0.6 \times 0.7 =$

   $0.06 \times 70 =$

   $60 \times 0.7 =$

   $420 \div 0.6 =$

2 Calculate. Write the missing numbers.

   a) $0.2 \times \boxed{} = 1.6$

   b) $8.4 = 7 \times \boxed{}$

   c) $3 \times \boxed{} = 0.8 \times \boxed{}$

   d) $8.75 \div \boxed{} = 1.75$

   e) $2.6 = \boxed{} \div 6$

   f) $9.2 = \boxed{} \div 5$

3 Roll a dice 4 times to generate 4 digits.
   Use them to fill the spaces.

   Aim to make the largest possible product.
   Now generate 4 digits to fit these spaces.

   $\boxed{}.\boxed{}\boxed{} \div \boxed{}$

   Aim to make the largest possible quotient.

Maths mastery

Dog food

Zena has four dogs. She buys dog food in 8.64 kg bags.
A bag of dog food lasts her 12 days.

- How much food do Zena's dogs eat between them each day?
  Give your answer in kilograms.

Show the method you used to solve the problem. Is it similar to or different from those used by your classmates?

Support notes
Provide children with base ten apparatus to help represent the problem using concrete materials. For example, discuss how they would split 8 thousands into 12 equal groups. (Exchange the 8 thousands into 80 hundreds and add the extra 6 hundreds to make 86 hundreds. These divide into 12 groups of 7 hundreds with 2 hundreds remaining. These are exchanged into 20 tens and with the 4 tens give 24 tens to be divided between the 12 groups.)

Problem solving

Reasoning skills
- Working systematically
- Using numerical reasoning to find different possible answers

Boat trip

A group of adults and children go on a boat trip around the island.
There is one more adult than the number of children in the group.
They pay a total of $60.70.

BOAT TRIP
ADULTS..........$7.45 each
CHILDREN.......$3.20 each

Your challenge
How many adults and children are in the group?
Another group of 4 people pay exactly $33. How many of the group are children?

Things to think about
- Could you estimate the numbers in the group as a rough answer?
- Can you think of a way to record totals in a list or table?
- How are you going to record your answers?
- Can you explain the methods you use?
- Would it help to have 'real' tickets or money to use?
- How can you make sure your answer is correct?
- **What do you notice** about the costs for the children as you write them out in a list?
- Can you see any patterns in the money amounts?
- **What is the same? What is different** about the totals for the children and the adults?

Show the method you used to solve the problem. Is it similar to or different from those used by your classmates?

Tips for success

This is an example of a two-stage 'finding all possibilities' problem and the children will need to be systematic and organised to solve it.

They need to work out the cost for different numbers of children and different numbers of adults. They then need to find two amounts that total $60.70. A further clue is that there is one more adult than the number of children.

It would help the children if they used a table to show the results of the cost for each increasing total amount.

Number	Children	Adults
1	$3.20	$7.45
2	$6.40	$14.90
3	$9.60	$22.35
4	$12.80	$29.80
5		
6		

This table shows totals for different numbers of children and adults. They can then look for pairs of totals that add to $60.70. They also know that there is one more adult than the number of children.

Using this information they should be able to work out that there are 6 adults and 5 children.

Try this

Support

Tickets with the prices of $3.20 and $7.45 can be provided for children to model the prices. They can then use trial and improvement for different totals, with the same rule of one more adult than the number of children. Give the children a labelled table for them to use to help them be systematic.

Extension

As this question has two variables, ask the children to use a matrix chart to present their results. Children's cost can be on one axis and adult's costs on the other so that the intersections show the totals for different combinations.

Children/Adults	1	2	3
1	$10.65	$13.85	$17.05
2	$18.10	$21.30	$24.50
3	$25.55	$28.75	$31.95

Progress notes

Please use this space to make your own notes.

3 Formulae and equations

Thinking starters

1 Answer these.

   a) $x = 8$

   Ari says, '$3x = 24$'.

   Ben says, '$3x = 38$'.

   Explain who is correct.

   b) $S = 4x + 6$

   The value of S is between 25 and 45. Work out the possible whole-number values for x.

   c) $T = y + 5$

   Ola says, 'The value of T could never be a negative number.'

   Is Ola correct? Explain your answer.

2 Ali uses a formula to represent lengths of rope.

   The total length of 2 pieces of rope a and 1 piece of rope b is equal to 3 pieces of rope c.

   Use this information to write an algebraic equation.

   Find possible lengths of rope a and rope b when rope c has the length 60 cm.

3 a) Write an algebraic expression to match the representation shown here.

   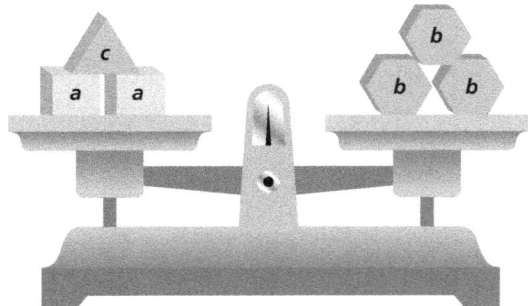

   b) What is the mass of b if $a = 180$ g and $c = 240$ g?

Maths mastery

Missing number problems

$6y + 4 = 46$

 Marta says that $y = 8$ Zena says that $y = 7$

- Is either of them correct? How do you know?

Show the method you used to solve the problem. Is it similar to or different from those used by your classmates?

Support notes
Use plastic cups (to represent unknown variables) and counters (to represent known numbers) to model the equation using physical materials, for example:

$6y + 4 = 46$

Discuss the possibilities if each cup contains 7 or 8 counters.

Problem solving

Reasoning skills
- Working systematically
- Spotting patterns
- Making generalisations

Planning a feast

Jessica is setting out tables in long lines in her school hall for a big Independence Day feast.

If the tables are arranged like this, she could set out 20 tables.

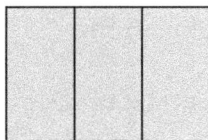

But if they are arranged like this, she could set out 12 tables.

One person can sit on each short side of a table, and 2 people at each long side.

- What is the largest number of people she could fit if she had 8 tables? How about 12?
- What about if she needed to fit 150 people? How many tables and rows would she need?

Things to think about
- Is there a link between the number of tables and the number of people who can be seated?
- How many more people could be seated for each table we add?
- **What do you notice** about the relationship between the number of tables and the number of people you can seat?
- **What is the same? What is different** about the two arrangements?
- If you know that 3 tables seat 10 people, **what else do you know?**
- **Convince me** that your formula works.

Your challenge

Create a formula for both ways of arranging the tables that will show how may people can be seated.

Show the method you used to solve the problem. Is it similar to or different from those used by your classmates?

Tips for success

The children use relationships to make general statements and then use these statements to develop basic algebraic formulae.

Ensure the children have prior experience of using letters to represent unknowns.

The children should also have prior experience of expressing generalised statements in words.

First, the children will need to specialise by working out how many people can be seated at each arrangement of tables. Arrangement 1 could seat 10 (2 + 1 + 1 + 1 + 1 + 1 + 1 + 2) and arrangement 2 could seat 14 (1 + 2 + 2 + 2 + 2 + 2 + 2 + 1).

The children should then extend this to more than 3 tables in a row and look for patterns and generalities, perhaps exploring 8 tables, which is suggested in the question.

After investigating a few specialised examples, children should try to create generalised statements in words, then use these to create formulae.

For arrangement 1: you can seat 2× the number of tables (1 either side of the table in the 'middle') + 4 (2 at each end). This leads to the formula $2n + 4$.

For arrangement 2: you can seat 4× the number of tables (2 either side of the tables in the 'middle') plus 2 (1 at each end). This leads to the formula $4n + 2$.

The children can then use these formulae to work out how many people they could seat with any number of tables. They should be encouraged to check their formula against their results earlier on in the activity.

The children can then attempt the last part of the problem (how many tables are needed to seat 150 people) through either trial and error using the formula, or by solving the equation ($2n + 4 = 150$, $4n + 2 = 150$), using a similar approach to that in the Missing numbers problem. (73 tables would be needed for arrangement 1 and 37 tables for arrangement 2.)

Try this

Support

The prompt could be re-created physically to give children practical experience. Additional tables could be added to each arrangement, with the children noting the change in the number of people that can be seated. Some less able children could express the relationship in words only.

Extension

The children could be challenged to create a formula that calculates how many rows are needed ($n \div 48$ and $n \div 52$), where n is equal to the total number of seats.

Progress notes

Please use this space to make your own notes.

4 Calculation problems

Thinking starters

1. Dan sells 36 computer games. He sells $\frac{1}{4}$ of them for $35 each and the rest for $30 each. How much money does he make?

2. What is the total mass of 1235 raspberries, each weighing 4 grams?

3. There are 38 shelves in the supermarket. Each shelf can hold 198 tins. If each shelf is stacked to full capacity, how many tins are there on the shelves altogether?

4. The length of a car journey from Kingston to Ocho Rios is 84 km.
   If Benita makes the journey from Kingston to Ocho Rios and back 15 times a year, how many kilometres does she travel?

5. There are 96 pages in a book. There are 45 questions on each page. How many questions are there in half the book?

6. The cost of buying a total of three flight tickets with Fly Airways is $199 cheaper than buying two flight tickets to the same destination with Star Choice Airline.
   No tickets cost less than $250.
   Find as many ways as you can to make this true.

Maths mastery

Solving problems with all four operations

Millie sets up a snack stall at playtimes.

- How many different ways are there to spend $100 at Millie's snack stall?

Millie spends $150 to make ten cups of orange juice. She then sells each for $20.

- For each cup of orange juice that she sells, how much money does she make?

Show the method you used to solve the problem. Is it similar to or different from those used by your classmates?

Support notes
Encourage children to view the problem as similar to finding combinations of 2, 3 and/or 5 that equal 10. Children should be able to add limited items to begin with. Ask: *How many cookies can you buy for one hundred dollars? Can you swap one of the cookies for something else?*

Children can use counters to share out $150 between ten cups to work out the $15 that each cup costs.

Problem solving

Reasoning skills
- Making connections
- Spotting patterns and relationships
- Making comparisons
- Using numerical reasoning

Would you rather ...?

What would you rather be given?
- $1 000 000 at the end of the year.
- 10 cents on the first day of the year, which doubles each following day for the rest of the year.
- $10 in the first week of the year, which then doubles each following week for the rest of the year.

Your challenge
Use the 'would you rather' statements to decide which would provide you with the most money over a year. Can you justify your answer?

Things to think about
- Which is the most efficient strategy to solve this problem?
- How will you record your answers?
- What do you notice about the amounts in the second and third options after day 10/week 10?
- Evaluate your choice. Are you sure it is the best option?

Show the method you used to solve the problem. Is it similar to or different from those used by your classmates?

Tips for success

Children investigate the value of three different quantities to determine which one they would rather have. They will need to use their mental and written calculation skills, such as constant addition versus constant doubling, to find solutions. They may use a calculator when the values become increasingly large.

Children will need to be systematic in their approach; for example, start at day 1 and then move to day 2 to double the amount. They will need to use discussion to establish any rules to enable to them to find a potential solution; for example, use constant doubling.

This activity will encourage children to use mathematical vocabulary such as quantity, addition, subtraction, multiplication and division. It will also encourage them to ask and answer questions explaining their reasoning.

Day	Amount	Week	Amount
1	10c	1	$10
2	20c (2 × 10c)	2	$20 (2 × $10)
3	40c (2 × 20c)	3	$40 (2 × $20)
4	80c (2 × 40c)	4	$80 (2 × $40)
5	...	5	...

Try this

Support
Children could use practical equipment such as base 10 or Dienes blocks to help them break up the problem and see the relationship between the amounts of money in the first few days/weeks of the second and third options. This may help them to predict the numbers as they become increasingly larger.

Extension
Children could create their own set of similar 'Would you rather ...?' statements.

Progress notes
Please use this space to make your own notes.

5 Algebra

Thinking starters

1 Write an expression for the *n*th term of these sequences. Use it to find the 20th term of each sequence.

   a) 7, 11, 15, 19, 23 …

   b) 10, 17, 24, 31, 38 …

2 Work out the 12th term in a sequence that uses the rule $6n - 4$.

3 Answer these.

   a) $2a + b = 16$

   Find the value of *a* when $b = 5$.

   b) $c \times d = 240$

   Find the value of *c* when $d = 10$.

   c) $e \div f = 6$

   Find the value of *e* when $f = 5$.

4 ◯ = 24

Find the value of ▢ in this equation.

◯ + ◯ = ◯ + ▢ + ▢ + ▢

5 $x + 4y = 60$ where *x* and *y* are both positive whole numbers.
Find possible values for *x* and *y*.

6 Jess buys some adult tickets for $6 each and some child tickets for $4 each. Jess spends $50.
How many of each kind of ticket did Jess buy?
Find two different possible answers.

Maths mastery

Equations with two unknowns

Ryan thinks of a number, multiplies it by 3 and then adds another number.
His answer is 28.
He writes down what he has done like this:

$3c + d = 28$
if $c = 1$ then d must $= 25$

- What other pairs of possible values for *c* and *d* can you find?

Show the method you used to solve the problem. Is it similar to or different from those used by your classmates?

Support notes
Use coloured cubes to physically represent Ryan's mystery numbers. For example:

▮ ▮ ▮ + ▢ = 28

Ask: *What could each dark cube be worth? What will the lighter cube need to be worth?* Encourage children to record their answers in a table.

Problem solving

Reasoning skills
- Spotting patterns and relationships
- Working systematically
- Making generalisations

Inspector Al Gebra investigates

Inspector Al Gebra is on the case of a burglar who is targeting Dotty Towers. There are 200 apartments there.

So far there have been 4 burglaries. They happened at apartment numbers 1, 3, 6 and 10. He looks at the dots on the front doors.

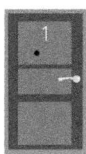 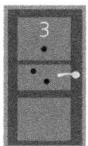 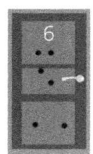 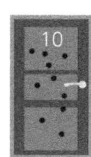

Things to think about
- Can you arrange the dots into shapes to spot any patterns?
- Which apartments will not be on the burglar's list? What are the reasons for this?
- Can you write the numbers in a list to help you work out the formula for finding any number in the pattern?
- Which is the odd one out: 4, 9, 15, 25, 36?
- Give me an example of a triangular number. **Another, another, another.**
- **Convince me** that x will be the next number in the sequence.
- **What's the link** between these rectangles of dots and the triangular numbers?

Your challenge

Which apartments will be targeted next if the burglar is allowed to continue until the pattern runs out?

Which apartment will be the 10th one targeted? How about the 15th?

Is there a formula that will help you to work out the nth apartment to be targeted?

Show the method you used to solve the problem. Is it similar to or different from those used by your classmates?

Tips for success

Children have to identify triangular numbers and identify the pattern to continue the number sequence.

Children may not be familiar with triangular numbers but it is more important that they spot the pattern and relationship between the numbers rather than recognise the terminology.

A triangular number is one that can produce similar right-angled triangles when placed as a series of dots (for example, 1, 3, 6, 10, 15, and so on).

```
1    3     6      10       15
o    o     o      o        o
     oo    oo     oo       oo
           ooo    ooo      ooo
                  oooo     oooo
                           ooooo
```

In this activity, children are encouraged to spot and continue the pattern to work out the nth number. This can be derived by doubling the triangular patterns into rectangles of dots:

```
n:  1    2      3       4        5
    ●o   ●●o    ●●●o    ●●●●o    ●●●●●o
         ●●o    ●●●o    ●●●●o    ●●●●●o
                ●●●o    ●●●●o    ●●●●●o
                n+1     ●●●●o    ●●●●●o
                                 ●●●●●o
```

The rectangle side lengths are n and $(n+1)$ so the formula for the rectangle is $n(n+1)$ and therefore the formula for the triangle is $\dfrac{n(n+1)}{2}$.

Encourage children to draw the dots in triangles and rectangles to enable them to spot this pattern in the numbers.

Try this

Support
Let children use counters to manipulate the 'dots' to see the patterns visually. Counters in two different colours can represent the rectangles used to find the formula for triangular numbers.

Extension
Encourage children to work through the problem individually or in pairs, without the step-by-step guidance. Can they spot the formula by themselves? Can they see a link to the rectangles of dots?

Progress notes
Please use this space to make your own notes.

6 Number problems

Thinking starters

1 Answer these.

  a) The difference between 3 and another number is 5.
  There are two possible other numbers. What are they?

  b) Ben says, 'Adding a number will always give a positive number answer.'
  Is Ben correct? Explain your answer.

2 Answer these calculations.

  4 + 2 = ☐   4 + −2 = ☐

  4 − 2 = ☐   4 − −2 = ☐

  What do you notice about the answers?

3 Copy this diagram.

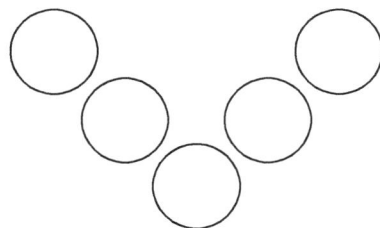

Place each of the numbers 1 to 5 in one of the circles.

Each diagonal of circles must have the same total.

How many possible ways can you do this?

What do you notice?

How can you be sure you have all the possibilities?

Maths mastery

Order of operations

Malik has answered this question in a test.

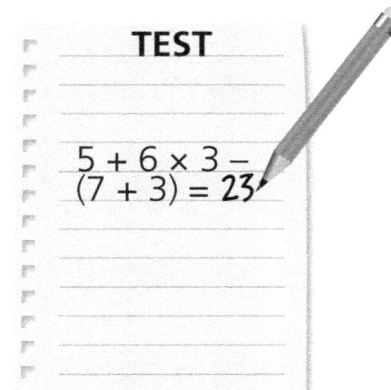

$5 + 6 \times 3 - (7 + 3) = 23$

- Is Malik correct? Explain how you know.

Show the method you used to solve the problem. Is it similar to or different from those used by your classmates?

Support notes

Recap the order of operations. It can be useful to indicate why having an order of operations is needed. You can do this by giving a simple calculation that could have different answers; for example, $6 \times 3 + 4 - 6 \div 2 = ?$ could have many different answers based on the order in which you carry out operations. Acronyms are best avoided as they do not give the full picture. Powers have priority, then multiplication/division, then addition/subtraction. Brackets jump to the head of the queue. Multiplications/divisions are calculated left to right, as are additions/subtractions.

Problem solving

Reasoning skills
- Working systematically
- Using numerical reasoning to find different possible answers

Magic squares

This is a magic square.

12	7	8
5	9	13
10	11	6

It is magic because each column, row and diagonal totals the same amount.
In this square, it totals 27.
We call this the magic number.

Things to think about
- Is there a link between the magic number and any number in the square?
- If we change the value of each digit by 1, would the square still be magic?
- **What do you notice** about the magic number/the total of the numbers in the magic square?
- Give me a **hard and an easy** magic square. What makes it hard/easy?
- If we know that this square is magic, **what else do we know?**

Your challenge
Create some magic squares.
Can you create a magic square just using the digits 1 to 9?
Can you use the magic squares you have created to create other magic squares?
Could you use algebra to help you?

Show the method you used to solve the problem. Is it similar to or different from those used by your classmates?

Tips for success

This problem is based on the classic magic square problem: the numbers in its rows, columns and diagonals all total to the same 'magic number'. They can vary in size. If one magic square has been 'discovered', an infinite number of linked magic squares can be created by changing each value in the square by a constant amount; for example, this magic square has been created by adding 4 to each number in the square.

16	11	12
9	13	17
14	15	10

In a 3 × 3 magic square, the magic number is always equal to 3× the number in the centre square. The total of the numbers in a 3 × 3 magic square is equal to 3× the magic number.

Magic squares can be expressed algebraically.

This square is magic as each row, column and diagonal has the total value $3n$. Further magic squares can be created algebraically and then an infinite number of 'related' squares can be created by substituting values for n.

$n + 3$	$n - 2$	$n - 1$
$n - 4$	n	$n + 4$
$n + 1$	$n + 2$	$n - 3$

For example, this square (each row/diagonal/column = $3n + 6$) can be used to create a magic square using digits 1–9 by substituting 3 for n.

$n - 1$	$n + 6$	$n + 1$
$n + 4$	$n + 2$	n
$n + 3$	$n - 2$	$n + 5$

Try this

Support

The children could create linked magic squares by using counters/cubes to represent the square and adding the same number of cubes/counters to each section and recording the related square.

Extension

The children should be encouraged to explore the algebraic representation of magic squares (see above).

Progress notes

Please use this space to make your own notes.

7 Multiplication

Thinking starters

1 Answer these.

   a) A biscuit factory makes 6700 biscuits in an hour. How many biscuits are made in 24 hours?

   b) A plane flies 3645 km twice a day for a week. How far did the plane fly altogether?

   c) A shop takes a delivery of 75 bags of dog food. Each bag weighs 2750 g. What is the total mass of dog food?

   d) Nishi calculates 3458 ÷ 91 = 38
   Use an inverse operation to check Nishi's calculation.

2 Daniel must choose boxes to pack 4800 tins. Boxes must hold at least 30 tins but no more than 60. All the boxes must be filled completely, with no spare tins.
Find three different ways Daniel could do this.

3 A supermarket needs 5000 bottles of drink. Packs hold 30 bottles. Alec says, '170 packs will be just enough.'
Is Alec correct? Explain your reasoning.

4 Sam calculated 537 × 24 by using long multiplication. He got the answer 3222. How do you know the answer must be wrong? What was his error? How would you explain to him where and why he went wrong?

Maths mastery

Buying mints

In each packet, there are 16 mints.

Shops buy the mints in large boxes containing 126 packets.

- How many mints are in each large box?

Large supermarkets can also buy the mints in Mega Crates.

Each Mega Crate contains 45 268 packets of mints.

- How many mints does a Mega Crate contain?

Show the method you used to solve the problem. Is it similar to or different from those used by your classmates?

Support notes

Use place-value cards to make the numbers 126 and 16. Encourage children to partition 16 and then multiply by each number separately (126 × 6 and 126 × 10).

Problem solving

Reasoning skills
- Conjecturing and convincing
- Spotting patterns and relationships
- Making connections
- Using numerical reasoning

Multiplication cubes

What if multiplication table facts were made up of three digits multiplied by each other, not two digits?

Would we have multiplication cubes?

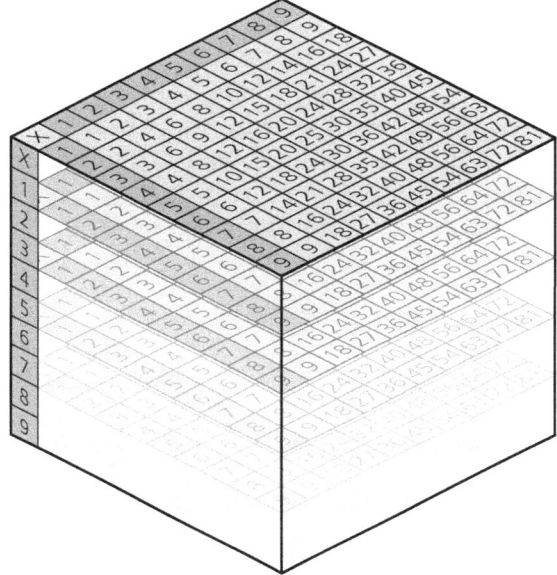

Here is the sort of fact that might be found in a multiplication cube.
It has been made by multiplying three different digits together.
2 × 3 × 5 = 30

- What other numbers can you make?

Things to think about
- Which numbers do you know you will definitely be able to make?
- Can you explain why some numbers are impossible to make?
- What are the factors of a number? Can you use these to help?
- Give me a **hard and an easy** number that you can make using three different digits.
- List the factors of the numbers you were not able to make. **What do you notice?**
- It is impossible to make 5, 11, 13 and 19 by multiplying three different digits. **What is the link between** these numbers?
- **If the answer is** 36, **what is the** multiplication **question** (with three different digits)?
- **Convince me** that it is impossible to make a prime number by multiplying three different digits.

Your challenge

How many of the numbers to 20 can you make by multiplying three different digits together?

What method have you used?

Before working out the answer, predict which numbers to 50 you will be able to make. Which will you not be able to make? Why?

Tips for success

Children explore the different numbers they can make by multiplying three different digits together.

The commutative property of multiplication states that any two numbers can be multiplied together to give the same result (a × b = b × a).

The associative property of multiplication deals with more than two numbers and states that the result will still be the same, regardless of which two numbers are multiplied first: (a × b) × c = a × (b × c).

In this investigation, children do not have to find all possible answers. Instead, they consider the numbers they cannot make and why this might be.

Children need to consider the factors of numbers they are able to make. So, 2 × 3 × 4 = 24 can be made by multiplying 6 × 4 × 1 (because 6 is equal to 2 × 3). Encourage children to use reasoning to explain the patterns and facts they find; for example, encourage them to consider what being a prime or a square number means for its factors (and therefore whether they can make it by multiplying a × b × c).

Try this

Support
Revise multiplication table facts. Ask children to explore the numbers they can make in a multiplication where one of them is the digit 1. Encourage them to make the link with table facts they have practised. Then let children explore numbers they can make when multiplying any three digits (not three different digits). Give them manipulatives to model their answers.

Extension
Encourage children to find alternative ways to make the same number and to investigate whether the number of factors a number has is related to the number of different ways they can make it using three different digits.

Progress notes

Please use this space to make your own notes.

8 Area and perimeter

Thinking starters

1. These shapes are drawn on a square grid. Each square represents 1 square centimetre. Calculate the perimeter of each shape.

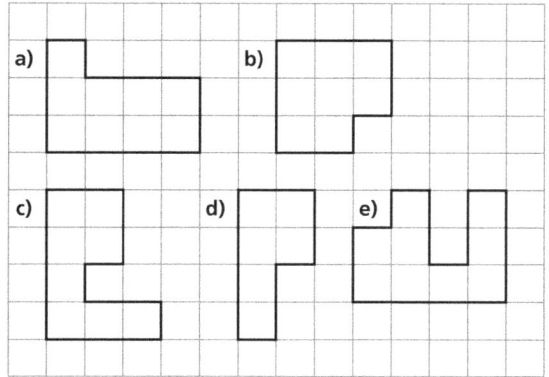

2. These shapes are drawn on a square grid. Each square represents 1 square centimetre. Calculate the area of each shape.

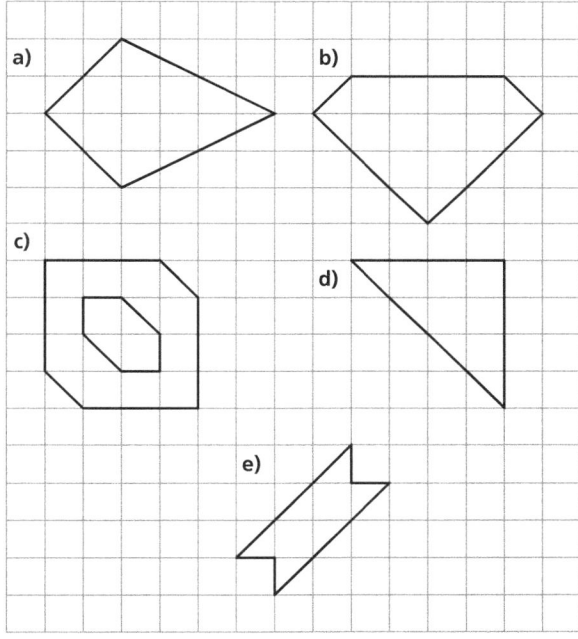

3. Calculate the perimeter and area of these triangles.

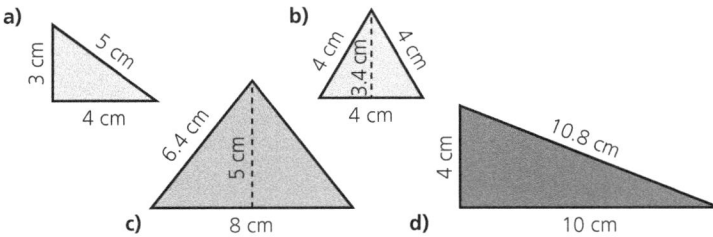

What do you notice about the answers for **a)** and **b)**?

What do you notice about the answers for **c)** and **d)**?

Maths mastery

Area and perimeter

A zoo has 36 m of fencing to build a new enclosure for its meerkats.

Meerkat enclosures have to be rectilinear. A rectilinear shape is made up from straight lines that meet at right angles. There are different rectilinear shapes that can be made with 36 m of fencing.

Bastian the Zoo Keeper says, 'As the perimeter of the enclosure will be 36 m, the area will be the same for each possible design.'

- Can you prove to Bastian that he is wrong, by showing him five possible enclosure designs and their areas?

Show the method you used to solve the problem. Is it similar to or different from those used by your classmates?

Support notes

Provide pentominoes or geoboards and rubber bands to enable children to explore the relationship between perimeter and area and the way that the perimeter can stay the same even though the area changes.

Problem solving

Reasoning skills
- Working systematically
- Spotting patterns

Chickens

Oak Farm raises free-range chickens and sells their eggs.

Free-range chickens need specific amounts of space.

Inside the coop: no more than 9 chickens per m².

Outside the coop: no more than 6 chickens per m².

Oak Farm is buying another 210 chickens that will need a new coop and outside enclosure. To keep the building work simple, the shapes will be rectangular or square.

Your challenge

Work out how much space the new coop and enclosures will take up.

Work out the minimum amount of wooden panels and chicken wire that would be needed for the enclosure and how much they would cost.

Find out how many chickens Oak Farm could fit on 70 m² of land.

2 m long wooden panels cost $200 each, with a further $20 per panel needed for the flat roof.

A 1 m long roll of chicken wire costs $350.

Things to think about
- How much space does each chicken take up inside and outside?
- How many m² of space does the farm need? Which way of enclosing this amount of space has the largest area?
- **What do you notice** about the amount of space the chickens need inside and out?
- **What is the same? What is different** between the different ways you could create an area of (xx m²)?
- **Convince me** that you have found the most chickens that could fit in 70 m².

Show the method you used to solve the problem. Is it similar to or different from those used by your classmates?

Tips for success

In this activity, children combine a number of areas of mathematics, including multiplicative reasoning, proportion, measures and area/perimeter. First, the children work out how much space is needed for 210 chickens, knowing that inside there can be no more than 9 chickens per m². and outside there must be no more than 6 chickens per m². Therefore we can work out the amount of space needed:

- inside: 210 ÷ 9 = 23 r3, so a total of 24 m² is needed
- outside: 210 ÷ 6 = 35, so a total of 35 m² is needed.

The children are then challenged to work out the smallest perimeters that enclose these areas. They should use their knowledge of the formula for the area of a rectangle and of factors to help them. They will see that:

- 24 m² could be achieved with the dimensions 24 × 1 (perimeter 50 m), 12 × 2 (perimeter 28 m) and 6 × 4 (perimeter 20 m)
- 35 m² could be achieved with the dimensions 35 × 1 (perimeter 72 m) or 7 × 5 (perimeter 24 m).

The children then work out the possible ways in which 70 m² could be used to build both a barn and outside enclosure, and which arrangement of barn versus outside space would house the greatest number of chickens.

The children could take a number of different approaches to solving this element, with trial and error likely to be the most common used.

Try this

Support

The children may benefit from using squared paper to create a scaled representation (with each square = 1 m²), for both parts of this problem.

Extension

Explain that new regulations specify that the chickens must have the same amount of space available inside and outside, that is, 6 chickens per m². Does the size of the barn have to increase by $\frac{1}{3}$?

Progress notes

Please use this space to make your own notes.

9 Three-dimensional shapes

Thinking starters

1 Gary has 36 centimetre cubes. He puts them together to make a cuboid. What could the length, width and height of the cuboid be?

2 This is the net of a cube. A cross (×) is drawn on one face of the cube.

What is the number of the face that will be opposite to the face marked with a cross?

3 A stripe is drawn round this cube.

Complete the stripe on this net of the cube.

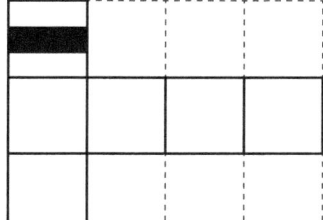

4 Nia builds a triangular prism. She says, 'My shape has no right angles.' Explain why Nia is incorrect.

5 On a 1–6 dice the numbers on opposite faces always add to 7.

Write the numbers 1 to 6 on this net of a dice so it is correctly numbered.

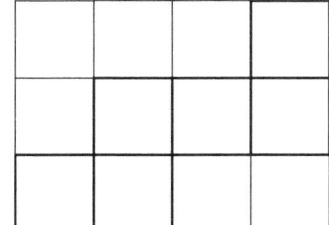

6 Which of these nets will make a 3-D shape? What shapes do they make?

a) 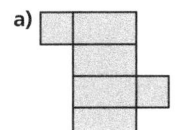 b) 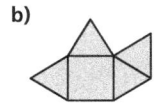 c) 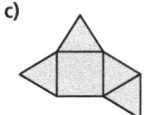 d)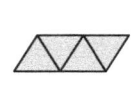

Maths mastery

Nets of 3-D shapes

Kai's class has been asked to make gift boxes by folding up nets.
They choose the shape of their gift boxes and have been given the following nets.

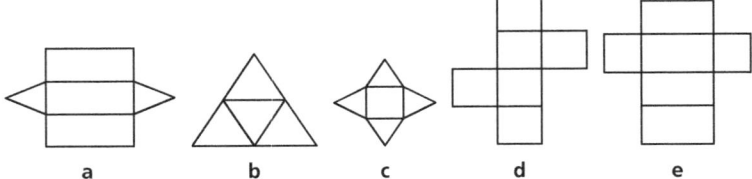

a   b   c   d   e

Kai wants to make a cube shaped gift box.
Jason wants to make a triangular-based pyramid shaped gift box.
Liam wants to make a triangular prism shaped gift box.

- Which of these nets should they each choose?

Show the method you used to solve the problem. Is it similar to or different from those used by your classmates?

Support notes
Provide 3-D models of the shapes to allow children to explore the different faces they are looking for. Foldable copies of the nets in the question may be useful as a way to get children to check their answers.

Problem solving

Reasoning skills
- Finding all possibilities
- Recognising patterns
- Making generalisations

Cube nets

When most people are asked to draw a net of a cube, they normally draw this net:

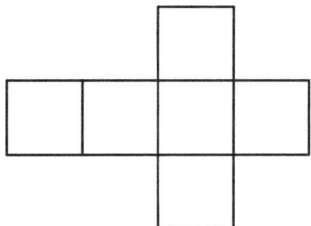

But there are more nets than this for a cube.

- Can you find out how many there are?

Remember: a net is a 2-D pattern of a 3-D shape, which can be folded to make a 3-D shape.

Your challenge
Find out all the different nets for a cube.

Things to think about
- How are you going to make sure you have found all the possibilities?
- How many squares will each net be made of? Why?
- Are there any arrangements of squares that will never make a cube?
- If we know the properties of a cube, **what else do we know** about the properties of a net for the cube?
- **What is the same? What is different** about the nets you have drawn?

Show the method you used to solve the problem. Is it similar to or different from those used by your classmates?

Tips for success

The children have to find all possible nets for a cube.
A net is a 2-D map of a 3-D shape which, when folded, makes that 3-D shape.
A cube has 11 nets in total, excluding rotations and reflections.
As a cube has 6 square faces, all the nets for a cube are made out of 6 squares.
The children will probably start this investigation by drawing possible nets for a cube (that is, drawing 6 squares in an arrangement). Squared paper will help their recording.

Try this

Support
The children could use modelling apparatus to construct a cube and then 'unfold' it into different nets.

Extension
The children could identify possible nets for a cuboid, looking for links with their cube nets. They could also place two shapes, (for example, a heart and star) on their nets to appear on the top/bottom of their cubes.

Progress notes

Please use this space to make your own notes.

10 Data

Thinking starters

1. These two pie charts compare the numbers of guests in two hotels.

   a) Compare the number of children at both hotels. Explain your reasoning.

   b) There were five more men than women at Beach Hotel. How many guests were men? Explain your reasoning.

   c) There were equal numbers of men and women at Sea Hotel. How many guests were men? Explain your reasoning.

   d) Show that the Sea Hotel had the higher number of women guests. Explain your reasoning.

   e) Estimate the angle of the sector representing men at the Beach Hotel. Explain clearly how you could check your answer.

2. The graph shows the height of a broad bean plant at the end of each week from when it is planted.

   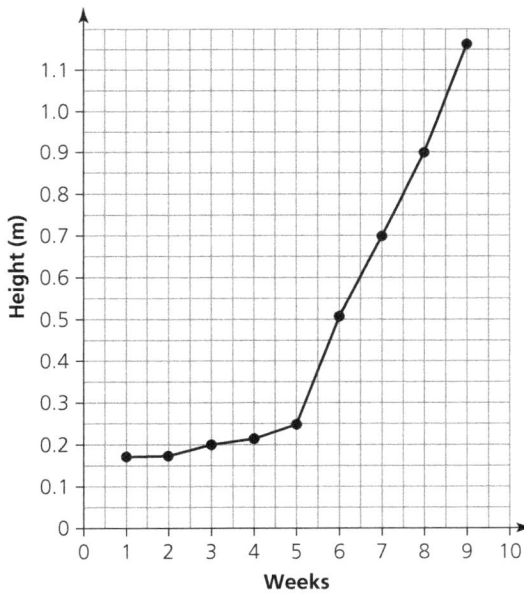

   a) What is its height in centimetres at the end of the third week?

   b) How many centimetres did the broad bean plant grow in the eighth week?

   c) How much, in metres, did the plant grow between the end of week 3 and the end of week 7?

   d) When did the plant first start growing much more rapidly?

Maths mastery

Pie charts

John owns an ice-cream shop. He asks 600 people what their favourite flavour of ice cream is so that he can order the right amount of ice cream.

He records his findings on a pie chart.

Favourite ice-cream flavour

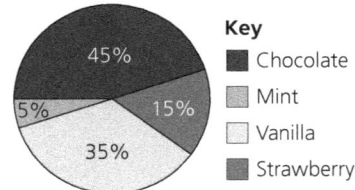

Key
- Chocolate
- Mint
- Vanilla
- Strawberry

- What is the most popular flavour of ice cream?
- How many people like strawberry ice cream the most?

Show the method you used to solve the problem. Is it similar to or different from those used by your classmates?

Support notes

When calculating 15%, encourage children to use their knowledge of 10% (and therefore 20%) to work out what halfway is.

One way of calculating the percentage quickly is to consider what is 15% of 100 (15), and then use this to derive what 15% of 600 will be.

Problem solving

Reasoning skills
- Making comparisons
- Interpreting and explaining information

Pies or lines?

We can display data in lots of different ways, including in pie charts and line graphs.

Each way of presenting data is particularly effective for certain types of data.

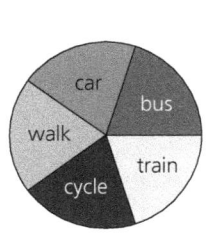 

Things to think about
- What type of data is best displayed in a pie chart? What type of data is best displayed on a line graph?
- How are you going to work most effectively? Will it be best for all of you to work on both investigations?
- Once you have carried out your investigation, what does your data show you?
- **What is the same? What is different** about a line graph and a pie chart?
- **What do you notice** about the type of data that is displayed on this graph/chart?
- **Convince me** this is the most effective way to display this data.
- Give me an idea of a data set to display on a line graph. **Another, another, another.**

Your challenge

In a group of four, plan and carry out two investigations.

For one investigation, you must present your data in a line graph.

For the other you must present your data as a pie chart.

Show the method you used to solve the problem. Is it similar to or different from those used by your classmates?

Tips for success

The children must consider the most useful type of data to display in pie charts and line graphs.

This investigation could easily be extended and combined with further investigation skills.

Revision of the main key skills of planning, carrying out and reporting on an investigation is included.

The children should have already worked with both pie and line charts before starting this investigation.

Pie charts show the relative proportion of data. They are most effectively used when comparing the sizes of different groups (for example, the most common way of getting to school).

Line graphs show the relationship between two sets of data. They are most effectively used for showing changes in data over a period of time (for example, to show the amount of water in a bath as it is being filled). They can also show other sets of data (for example, the rate of growth of bacteria versus temperature).

Try this

Support
The children may benefit by having one of the steps for the investigation outlined for them.

Extension
The children could be encouraged to explore other ways of presenting data and which data types are most effectively displayed using these. The level to which the children are expected to interpret the data they have collected should also be significantly higher for more able children.

Progress notes

Please use this space to make your own notes.

11 Mental calculation

Thinking starters

1 Cans of beans come in three sizes.

   A 450 g tin costs 70c   A 200 g tin costs 40c   Four 400 g tins together cost $2

   What is the cheapest way for Chad to buy 1 kilogram of beans?

2 A bus fare normally costs $3.
   There are some special offers.

   Two tickets for $5   Three tickets for $8   Six tickets for $14

   What is the cheapest way to buy 12 tickets?

3 Manisha has five parcels that together weigh 23 kg.

   Parcel A + Parcel B = 8 kg   Parcel B + Parcel C = 10 kg

   Parcel C + Parcel D = 9 kg   Parcel D + Parcel E = 8 kg

   What does each parcel weigh?

4 Mrs Jones makes a booklet. Black and white pages cost 3 cents each and colour pages cost 8 cents each.
   The booklet costs 76 cents. How many black and white pages and how many colour pages could there be in it?

5 Leta has 100 football stickers. She gives a fifth of them to Hannah, a quarter of the remainder to Ryan and 26 to Jayden. How many stickers does Leta have left?

Maths mastery

Mixed mental calculations

A teacher has asked a class to carry out the following calculation mentally:

Keira says that you cannot do the calculation mentally.

- Can you explain to Keira how you can carry out the calculation mentally?

Show the method you used to solve the problem. Is it similar to or different from those used by your classmates?

Support notes

The use of Gattegno charts (see page 6) and place-value cards is useful for revisiting the partitioning of numbers.

Demonstrate how multiplication is distributive, that is, 63 × 6 = (60 × 6) + (3 × 6). Use arrays to help children visualise this.

Problem solving

Reasoning skills
- Making generalisations
- Spotting patterns

Greatest product

If you take the number 10 and split it into two numbers, then multiply them together, you could create a large range of products.

For example, 1 × 9 = 9, 2 × 8 = 16, 3 × 7 = 21, etc.

- Which way of splitting 10 and then multiplying would give you the greatest product?
- Is this the same if you start with any number and split this number into two numbers?
- What would give the greatest product if you split your starting number into three numbers?

Your challenge
Investigate how to create the greatest number product by splitting the starting number into two and multiplying.

Things to think about
- Which number are you going to start with?
- Which way of splitting has given you the greatest product?
- Is this the same for all starting numbers? Does the same rule apply for odd and even numbers?
- How will you use what you have learned about splitting numbers into two numbers to investigate how to form the greatest product by splitting your starting number into three numbers?
- **What is the same? What is different** about these two ways of splitting this number/about the ways you have achieved the greatest product for these (two or more) numbers?
- **Convince me** that this will always produce the greatest product.
- Is it **always, sometimes or never true** that there is only ever one way to achieve the greatest product?
- **What do you notice** about the split of numbers that gives you the greatest product?

Tips for success

Children investigate the greatest product (the result of multiplying two or more numbers together) they can make by splitting a number into two or more parts; for example, splitting 10 into 7 and 3 to make a product of 21.

When splitting a number into two, the maximum product is found:

- if the number is even: when both numbers are equal; for example, the greatest product that can be found by splitting 10 into two numbers is 25: 5 × 5
- if the number is odd: when the 'split' numbers differ by 1; for example, for 9, the greatest product is 20 (5 × 4).

Splitting the number into two can be linked to finding the area of a rectangle, where the length and width total the whole number.

When a number is split into three, the greatest product is formed:

- if the number is even: when all numbers are equal (for example, for 24, 8 × 8 × 8)
- if the number is odd: when all the numbers differ by 1 except where the number can be split into three equal parts.

Splitting a number into three can be linked to finding the volume of a cuboid. (Children's familiarity with finding the volume of a cuboid will determine if this is a useful link to make.)

Try this

Support
The children may benefit from using squared paper to represent the arrays/rectangles formed and their resulting products when splitting a number into two.

Extension
Ask the children to investigate how they can make the biggest product if they could split a number into as many ways as they want (the biggest product will always be from a combination of 2s and 3s). The children could also explore if the conjectures and generalisations they have made are still true if they are allowed to have decimal numbers or fractions as part of their split.

Progress notes

Please use this space to make your own notes.

12 Multiples, factors and primes

Thinking starters

1 Answer these.

a) List all the factor pairs of 72.

b) Write the missing factors of 70.

1 ☐ 5 7 10 ☐ 35 ☐

c) List all the numbers that are factors of 30 and multiples of 5.

d) What is the highest common factor of 18 and 9?

e) Write down all the common factors of 12, 24 and 45.

f) Find the lowest common multiple of 5, 6, 8 and 12.

2 Write down the prime numbers:

a) between 70 and 80

b) between 100 and 110.

3 Dev divides numbers by prime numbers:

36 ÷ 3 = 12   50 ÷ 5 = 10

Dev says, 'When I divide a number by a prime number, the answer is not prime.'
Is this always, sometimes or never true?

Maths mastery

Factors

Melissa is looking at the factors of the following numbers:

10, 18, 15, 19

- Which number is the odd one out? Why?

Show the method you used to solve the problem. Is it similar to or different from those used by your classmates?

Support notes

Ensure children understand the definition of a factor as two whole numbers that multiply together to make the 'target' number. Introduce children to finding factors systematically by starting with 1 and the number, then looking to see if 2 is a factor (and what its pair is), then 3, and so on, until there are no new numbers.

Begin to explore the number of factors for different numbers, introducing children to prime (and square) numbers.

Recording using 'factor bugs' can help, and it draws attention to different types of numbers (for example, prime numbers – which only have 'two legs' – and square numbers that have an odd number of 'legs').

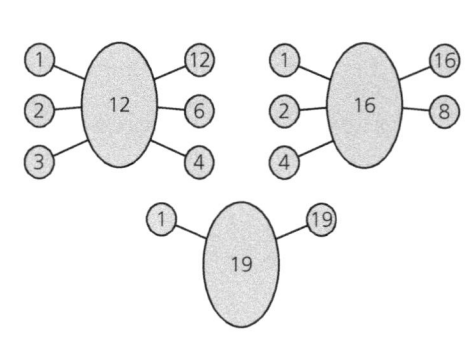

Problem solving

Reasoning skills
- Working systematically
- Solving problems
- Finding all possibilities

Perfect, deficient and abundant numbers

Mathematicians love categorising numbers.
One way is into 'perfect', 'deficient' and 'abundant' numbers.

The numbers are placed into these categories based on something to do with their factors, but it is not related to simply how many factors a number has.

Here are some numbers, their factors and their category.

6	1, 2, 3, 6	Perfect
12	1, 2, 3, 4, 6, 12	Abundant
30	1, 2, 3, 10, 15, 30	Abundant
16	1, 2, 4, 8, 16	Deficient
26	1, 2, 13, 26	Deficient

Your challenge
Work out what makes a number perfect, abundant or deficient.
Are there more abundant, perfect or deficient numbers under 50?

Things to think about
- How are you going to record your answers?
- How are you going to make sure you have found all the factors for each number?
- What makes a number abundant, deficient or perfect?
- Are there any links or patterns that help you predict which category a number will fall into?
- **What do you notice** about the perfect number 6? What are its factors? What happens when you add the factors together?
- **What do you notice** about (a deficient number)? What are its factors? What happens when you add the factors together?
- If you know that 6 is a perfect number, can you use this fact to help you find any abundant numbers?

Tips for success

Children are asked to investigate perfect, abundant and deficient numbers.

A secure knowledge of factors of numbers is needed for this activity. (Factors of numbers are numbers that can multiply together to make the target number; for example, the factors of 15 are 1, 3, 5 and 15 and are usually recorded in pairs, for example 1 and 15, 3 and 5. Factors can be shown using arrays, for example 3 and 5.

Numbers are placed into these categories based on the sum (total) of their factors.

- **Perfect numbers:** the sum of all the factors of a number, excluding the number itself, is EQUAL to the number. There are only two perfect numbers under 50: 6 and 28.
- **Abundant numbers:** the sum of all the factors of a number, excluding the number itself, is more than the number itself. For example, 12 is the first abundant number: its factors are 1, 12, 2, 6, 3, 4 and $1 + 2 + 6 + 3 + 4 = 16$.
- **Deficient numbers:** the sum of all the factors of a number, excluding the number itself, is less than the number itself. For example, 16 is deficient: the factors of 16 are 1, 16, 2, 8, 4 and $1 + 2 + 8 + 4 = 15$.

There are more deficient numbers under 50: there are 39 deficient, 9 abundant and 2 perfect numbers.

All multiples of perfect numbers are abundant. All abundant numbers under 50 are even (the first odd abundant number is 945!).

Try this

Support

Initially, the children should focus on all numbers under 30. They could be provided with a list of factors for most numbers under 30 to use to classify into perfect, abundant or deficient. Alternatively, if the children still need work on finding all factors of numbers, this could become the main focus of this activity, perhaps combining with a more able child who can explore if the numbers are abundant, deficient or perfect and begin to look for patterns.

Extension

The children can extend their investigation beyond 50 and describe their patterns so that they are able to predict if a number will be perfect, abundant or deficient.

Progress notes

Please use this space to make your own notes.

13 Fractions

Thinking starters

1 Answer these.

   a) Fay simplifies $\frac{48}{60}$. She says, '$\frac{48}{60}$ simplified to its lowest terms is $\frac{24}{30}$'.

   Is Fay correct? Explain your answer.

   b) Which fraction is the odd one out?

   $\frac{12}{32}$ $\frac{15}{40}$ $\frac{18}{50}$ $\frac{21}{56}$ $\frac{30}{80}$

   Explain your answer.

   c) Ola says, 'All fractions with an even numerator can be simplified by dividing by 2.'

   Is Ola correct? Explain your answer.

2 Answer these.

   a) Write a fraction that is larger than $\frac{5}{6}$ and smaller than $\frac{11}{12}$.

   b) These fractions are in order.

   $\frac{3}{5}$ $\frac{5}{8}$ $\frac{13}{20}$

   State the order and explain how you know.

3 Answer these.

   a) What number is $2\frac{1}{2}$ more than $3\frac{5}{6}$?

   b) Nia has some counters. She says, '$\frac{1}{4}$ are blue, $\frac{5}{12}$ are yellow and $\frac{1}{3}$ are green. The rest of the counters are red.'
   Explain why Nia must be wrong.

   c) Find two fractions that have a difference of $\frac{1}{2}$.

   d) Find two fractions that have a total of $2\frac{1}{4}$.

Maths mastery

Comparing and ordering fractions

Put the following fractions in order of size, starting with the smallest.

$\dfrac{10}{12}$ $\dfrac{3}{4}$ $\dfrac{3}{8}$ $\dfrac{7}{8}$ $\dfrac{2}{12}$

- How do you know?

Show the method you used to solve the problem. Is it similar to or different from those used by your classmates?

Support notes
Children can use a fraction wall (that shows quarters, eighths and twelfths) to help compare the fractions visually.

This will also help children to convert $\dfrac{3}{4}$ into eighths. Number rods may also support understanding.

Problem solving

Reasoning skills
- Working systematically
- Solving problems
- Conjecturing and convincing

Monsters

For this challenge you will need a selection of coloured interlocking cubes. Each cube is worth the value shown below.

Red = $\frac{3}{8}$ Green = $1\frac{1}{2}$

Blue = $\frac{3}{4}$ Brown = $\frac{3}{16}$

Yellow = $\frac{15}{16}$ Black = $\frac{1}{4}$

Your challenge
Build a monster out of cubes.
All the cubes in your monster must total $15\frac{1}{2}$ and include each colour of cube.

Things to think about
- How are you going to make sure your monster has the correct total?
- What do you need to do to add these fractions together?
- How many different ways are there to make a monster that totals $15\frac{1}{2}$ if the cubes have the values that are shown on the left?
- Can you create a new monster by exchanging cubes?
- **What do you notice** about the cube values?
- Give me a way of making $1\frac{1}{2}$ using these cubes. **Another, another, another.**
- **Convince me** that your monster will/does add up to the target value.

Show the method you used to solve the problem. Is it similar to or different from those used by your classmates?

Tips for success

Using a selection of coloured interlocking cubes, children are asked to create a monster. Each cube is assigned a value and the children have a target of $15\frac{1}{2}$ that their monster must be worth.

The problem requires a secure knowledge of addition of fractions, including converting to equivalent fractions. For the children who are not confident with adding fractions with mixed denominators they can start with cubes that have the same denominator, with one mixed number.

Fractions with the same denominator can be added simply by adding the numerators together. Fractions with different denominators can be added by converting each fraction so that the fractions share a common denominator, for example $\frac{3}{4} + \frac{3}{8} = \frac{6}{8} + \frac{3}{8} = 1\frac{1}{8}$.

Try this

Support
The values provided can be edited so that this activity is accessible for all the children in your class. Ensure they have access to a wide range of representations to help them calculate the totals.

Extension
Add additional constraints to the activity; for example, say that only one green cube can be used, or that a minimum of four brown cubes must be used.

Progress notes
Please use this space to make your own notes.

14 Fractions, decimals, percentages

Thinking starters

1 Answer these.

  a) Amanda sat two tests. She scored:

  17 out of 20 in Maths   21 out of 25 in English

  Write her scores as percentages.

  b) Which is largest of these numbers?

  45%   0.6 $\frac{3}{25}$

2 Answer these.

  a) Jessica scored 18 out of 25, 70% and $\frac{15}{20}$ in three tests.

  Explain which is Jessica's best score.

  b) Tyler ate $\frac{1}{6}$ of a pizza. He tried to write this as a percentage, but couldn't get an exact answer.

  Advise Tyler what he should do.

  c) Alec got between 5% and 10% of the questions in a test wrong. There were 40 one-mark questions. How many questions could Alec have got wrong?

  Explain your answer.

  d) Write three decimals between $\frac{1}{8}$ and $\frac{3}{8}$. Explain your answer.

Maths mastery

Fractions, decimals and percentages

- Can you match the decimal fractions to their fraction equivalents?
- Complete the table below, which shows fraction, decimal and percentage equivalencies.

Fraction	Decimal	Percentage
$\frac{3}{4}$		
	0.30	
		66%
$\frac{1}{5}$		

Show the method you used to solve the problem. Is it similar to or different from those used by your classmates?

Support notes

Use blank 100 squares and plastic counters to practise modelling equivalent relationships between fractions, decimals and percentages. Ask children what each square is worth $\left(\frac{1}{100}\right)$ and what each complete row is worth $\left(\frac{1}{10}\right)$.

Use a number line from 0 to 1 and mark equivalent fractions, percentages and decimals or draw bar models to show equivalents.

Show children combinations of equivalent values so that they can spot the relationships.

Problem solving

Reasoning skills
- Solving problems
- Making connections
- Convincing

Fraction maths maze race

This is a maths maze.
You can move one square at a time left, right, up or down.
Roll a dice to get a start number.

Start	$+1\frac{1}{4}$	-0.5	$+\frac{10}{4}$	$+2\frac{6}{8}$
$+1.25$	$-\frac{1}{2}$	$+\frac{3}{2}$	$-1\frac{2}{8}$	$+0.125$
$-1\frac{4}{12}$	-0.75	$+\frac{3}{12}$	-2.5	$+\frac{1}{4}$
-0.25	$+\frac{10}{8}$	$+\frac{6}{4}$	-2.25	$+2\frac{1}{2}$
$+\frac{9}{12}$	$\times 2$	$+\frac{3}{4}$	$+100\%$	Finish

Your challenge

What is the smallest total you can make as you go through the maze from the start to the finish?

What is the largest total you can make?

What do you think is the best route through the maze? Why?

Things to think about
- How will you add and subtract using fractions and decimals? Will you convert the amounts to either fractions or decimals?
- Can you find common denominators to help?
- Can you use equivalent fractions to help?
- **What is the same? What is different** about $1\frac{1}{4}$ and 1.25?
- **What do you notice** about finding the route through the maze that gave you the smallest/largest total?

Tips for success

Children use their knowledge of fractions, decimals and percentages to find a way through a maths maze to find the smallest and largest totals.

Prior to this activity, children will need to have experienced using fractions, decimals and percentages.

Fraction calculations are challenging; if the fractions that are to be added or subtracted have different denominators (for example, $\frac{1}{2}$ and $\frac{1}{8}$) children will need to convert the fractions so that they have a common denominator.

The numbers in the maze include mixed numbers and improper fractions. Children will need to decide how to add each type of number (for example, convert mixed numbers into improper fractions, then find a common denominator before adding or subtracting).

The maze also includes decimal fractions. All the decimals, when converted into fractions, have denominators of either 2, 4, 8 or 12. These can be added to the other fractions once a common denominator is found.

Children may decide which route to take based on how easy the calculation will be. However, the challenge of finding the largest and smallest totals through the maze will force them to look for alternative routes.

Try this

Support
Encourage children to work with physical representations of fractions such as fraction circles and fraction towers, with decimals marked as well as fractions. Children can manipulate these resources to solve the calculations.

Extension
Add a different challenge such as finding a route through the maze that achieves a total as close to 10 as possible. Children can also create their own mazes to challenge a friend.

Progress notes

Please use this space to make your own notes.

15 Percentages

Thinking starters

1 Work out these percentages.

   a) 5% of $73

   b) 10% of $73

   c) 15% of $73

   d) 20% of $73

2 Answer these.

   a) Jan has $98. He spends 25% of his money on clothes and 35% on food.
      How much does Jan have left?

   b) 100% of 250 = 250.
      Find 200% of 250.

   c) 25% of a number is 38.
      What is the number?

3 75% of a number is 600.
   What is the number?
   Show how you completed this calculation.

4 Work out three possible solutions for this statement.

   ☐% of ☐ = 40

5 Two jars each have a different number of counters, but they both have the same number of red counters. Work out the missing percentage.

   Jar 1: 200 counters with 15% red

   Jar 2: 500 counters with ☐% red

Maths mastery

Percentage problems

The following items are on sale.

- Which item has the most money off? How do you know?

Show the method you used to solve the problem. Is it similar to or different from those used by your classmates?

Support notes

Encourage children to use facts they do know to help with facts they do not. Show children this sort of table.

100%	10%	1%	50%	5%

Provide children with plenty of practice at completing the table quickly and show that any percentage can be found using the information it contains.

Problem solving

Reasoning skills
- Conjecturing and convincing
- Making connections
- Using numerical reasoning

Grade 6, we have a problem!

The crew on a spaceship has radioed down to Earth with a problem: their fuel gauge is broken.

Total fuel cells: 360 | Percentage left: 50% | Number of fuel cells left: ERROR

The fuel gauge shows the *total amount* of fuel cells (which is always 360), the *percentage* of fuel cells that are left and the *number* of fuel cells that are left.
As the gauge is broken, the astronauts can see the percentage, but they do not know the exact number of fuel cells that are left.

- Can you help?

Your challenge

Without writing out every possible percentage, can you write a set of instructions that will help the astronauts work out the number of fuel cells for all the different percentages of 360?

You can only include three steps.

There may be several ways you can work out the amount left, but try to find the quickest way: when you are steering a spaceship travelling at 8 km per second, time is precious!

Things to think about
- What does it mean to find the percentage of an amount?
- Can you rewrite the broken fuel gauge as if it were a missing number question?
- How would you find 50% of 360? Can you think of another way to do this?
- What strategy would you use to find 15% of 360? **Another, another, another**.
- Give me a **hard and an easy** percentage of 360.
- If we know what 10% of a number is, **what else do we know**?
- What is the **quickest and easiest** way to find 12% of a number?

Tips for success

Children investigate ways of calculating percentages of amounts and devise a set of instructions to help a space crew do this quickly.

A percentage is a way to express an amount as part of a whole, relating it to the number 100 (from the Latin per centum, which means 'by the 100'). It is expressed using the symbol %.

There are several ways to calculate percentages, all using numerical reasoning; for example, to find 50% of 360:

- 50 is half of 100, so the amount should be divided by 2.
- To find 10%, the amount should be divided by 10. Five tens make 50, so the answer should then be multiplied by 5.
- Another more convoluted way is to find 5% and then multiply by 10.

The aim is for children to explore different strategies and choose the most efficient method, explaining their decisions.

This investigation references the 'square peg in a round hole' air filter that needed to be invented by NASA for the Apollo 13 crew, using only the equipment that was available on-board.

Try this

Support

For those less confident working with percentages, alter the numbers involved. Ask children to colour 50 squares out of 100 and establish that this is the same as a half and 50%. Explore ways to find 50% of different numbers (for example, sharing objects into two equal groups, dividing by 2).

Extension

Children could design a percentage helper as a pie chart showing the fuel cells for 50%, 25%, 10%, 9%, 5% and 1%. These add to 100% and, as the total number of fuel cells is 360, children should be able to calculate percentages and use the corresponding angles to draw their pie chart. For example, 50% of 360 is 180, so the angle to show 50% is 180°.

Progress notes

Please use this space to make your own notes.

16 Ratio and proportion

Thinking starters

1 Alec gets 3 questions wrong for every 7 questions he gets right.

a) If he has 21 questions wrong, how many questions does Alec have right?

b) If he has 14 questions right, how many questions does he have wrong?

2 Mia buys 4 oranges for $1.20.

a) How much would 12 oranges cost?

b) How much would 5 oranges cost?

3 There are 5 white beads for every 3 blue beads.

a) Shivana has 60 white beads. How many blue beads does she have?

b) Kia has 60 blue beads. How many white beads does she have?

c) What fraction of the beads are white?

4 Answer these.

a) Raj mixes 15 kg of sand with 4 kg of cement. How many kilograms of sand will he mix with 20 kg of cement?

b) Five music downloads cost $17. How much would six music downloads cost?

c) An adult ticket costs $1\frac{1}{2}$ times as much as a child's ticket. If an adult's ticket costs $12, what is the cost of a child's ticket? Explain your reasoning.

d) In a bag there are 5 pieces of fruit. Three are apples and the rest are pears. What is the ratio of apples to pears in the bag? Explain your reasoning.

e) Large tins of peas cost 75 cents and small tins cost 55 cents. Jill spends $8.75 on some large and small tins of peas. How many tins did she buy altogether?

Maths mastery

Ratio problems

The recipe below makes enough strawberry cupcakes for four people.

Flour	135 g
Butter	90 g
Sugar	150 g
Eggs	2
Fresh cream	30 ml
Strawberries	100 g

I want to make enough cupcakes for 12 people.

- How much of each ingredient do I need?

Show the method you used to solve the problem. Is it similar to or different from those used by your classmates?

Support notes

Children can use a table to help build up the recipe (or one ingredient from it) to help understand how to convert the measurements. For example:

Number of people recipe serves	Amount of eggs needed	How did you find the amount?
4	2 eggs	Recipe amount
8	4 eggs	Recipe amount × 2
12	6 eggs	Recipe amount × 3

Use this to derive the method (× 3) and then calculate the other amounts without the use of a table.

Problem solving

Reasoning skills
- Conjecturing and convincing
- Making connections
- Using numerical reasoning

Raspberry cupcakes

Here is a recipe chart to make different numbers of raspberry cupcakes.

	1 cake	3 cakes	6 cakes	12 cakes	18 cakes	x cakes
Flour				140 g		
Butter			60 g			360 g
Sugar						420 g
Large eggs		1			6	
Dried raspberry pieces				$\frac{1}{4}$ of a 240 g packet		$\frac{3}{4}$ of a 240 g packet
Raspberry flavourings				$\frac{1}{2}$ a teaspoon		

As you can see, some of the measurements are missing!

Your challenge

Complete the recipe table above.

Then, if Mary wanted to make x number of cakes, can you work out how much of each ingredient she would need?

Things to think about
- What is the relationship between the number of cakes and the amount of ingredients?
- Would it be best to work out all the ingredients for one of the quantities of cakes first?
- **Convince me** that this is the correct value for this section.
- If we know that we need 140 g of flour for 12 cakes, **what else do we know?**

Tips for success

The children need to identify and use the proportional relationship between different quantities to work out the amount of ingredients required to make different numbers of cupcakes.

The quantities are all proportional to each other and to the number of cakes that they make.

The children need to understand that if 12 cakes need 140 g of flour, then 3 cakes will need 35 g, as 12 is 4 times 3, therefore 12 cakes will need 4 times as much flour.

The children also need a secure understanding of the inverse relationships between operations.

The values chosen for some of the ingredients will require knowledge of multiplication and division of fractions.

Try this

Support

The children should be provided with physical representations, such as cubes, to help them explore the relationships between quantities in this problem. The children who are very insecure at multiplying/dividing fractions may prefer to convert the dried raspberry pieces to grams and to leave the amount of flavouring needed.

Extension

The extra challenge task encourages children to use the information they have found out in a slightly different way. The children could also be encouraged to express the proportions in the problem as ratios.

Progress notes

Please use this space to make your own notes.

17 Area of shapes

Thinking starters

1 Answer these.

   a) A triangle has an area of 80 cm² and a height of 5 cm.
      What is the length of the base of the triangle?

   b) Nia says, 'My rectangle has an area of 40 cm² and a perimeter of 82 cm.'
      What is the length and width of Nia's rectangle?

   c) Gregor says, 'This parallelogram has an area of 180 cm².'
      Is Gregor correct? Explain your answer.

   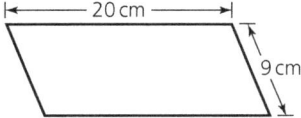

2 Answer these.

   a) This rectangle is made from two triangles and a parallelogram. The area of each triangle is 12 cm².

   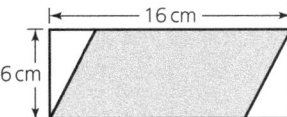

   What is the area of the shaded parallelogram?

   b) Chad says, 'If I make rectangles and squares with the same area, the square will always have the smaller perimeter.'
      Is Chad always, sometimes or never correct?

Maths mastery

What is the area?

Joshua has made this shape out of a parallelogram and a triangle.

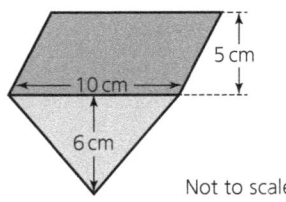

Not to scale

- What is the area of Joshua's shape?

Show the method you used to solve the problem. Is it similar to or different from those used by your classmates?

Support notes
Provide children with the relevant formulae and discuss the value of each variable.
To help embed the formulae show why each works, using squared paper and a pair of scissors.
Show how a parallelogram is simply a rectangle rearranged as follows:

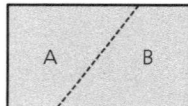 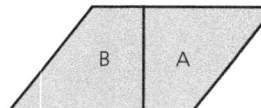

Problem solving

Reasoning skills
- Making generalisations
- Making connections
- Spotting patterns

Formulae

You know the formula for the area of a triangle:
　　area = length × width
Or, if we called the length *a* and the width *b*:
　　area = *a* × *b*.
Is there a formula to find the area of other shapes?

Your challenge

Investigate if there is a formula for the area of any other 2-D shapes, starting with a triangle, parallelogram and trapezium.

Remember: area is a measure of the space a shape or object takes up.

Things to think about
- How are you going to try to identify if there is a formula?
- Does your formula work for all types of shapes? Even peculiar ones?
- Can you use the formula for a rectangle to help you investigate if there is a formula for these other shapes too?
- **What is the same? What is different** between a rectangle and square?
- **Convince me** that this is the formula for the area of your shape.
- **What do you notice** if you duplicate this triangle/parallelogram/trapezium?
- Could you split the parallelogram into two equal triangles?

Show the method you used to solve the problem. Is it similar to or different from those used by your classmates?

Tips for success

Children investigate formulae for finding the area of different shapes.

The children should know that the formula for the area of a rectangle is area = length × width, which can be expressed algebraically as area = $a \times b$ if a is length and b is width.

The formula for the area of a rectangle can be used to develop the formulae for other shapes.

- **Triangle:** the formula for the area of a triangle is $\frac{1}{2}$ (base × height).
- **Parallelogram:** the formula for the area of a parallelogram is base × height.
- **Trapezium:** the area of a trapezium can be expressed as $\frac{1}{2}$ (base 1 + base 2) × height.

Try this

Support

Provide paper and scissors and ask children to cut out shapes with the same lengths so the shapes can be compared. Encourage children to cut the shapes so that rectangles can be seen and compared. For example, show that any two triangles the same size have the same area as a rectangle. This can then be related to the formula for area of a triangle.

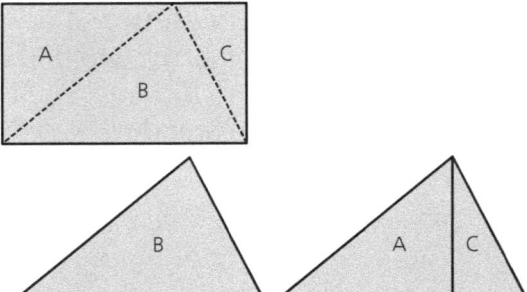

Extension

The children should be encouraged to ensure they can prove their formulae and to ensure the formulae work for all types of triangle/trapezium/parallelogram.

Progress notes

Please use this space to make your own notes.

18 Volume

Thinking starters

1 Answer these.

   a) Find the volume of this cuboid.

   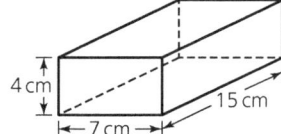

   b) A cube has a side length of 6 cm. What is the volume of the cube?

   c) A cuboid is 25 cm long, 12 cm wide and 8 cm high. What is the volume of the cuboid?

   d) The area of the shaded face of this cuboid is 38.5 cm². The longest side is 12 cm. What is the volume of the cuboid?

   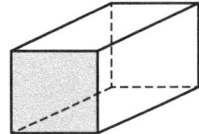

   e) The area of the base of a cuboid is 150 cm² and its height is 7 cm. What is the volume of the cuboid?

   f) A cube has a volume of 125 cm³. What is the length of one side?

2 Answer these.

   a) Nia says, 'If a cube has a volume of 100 cm³, it must be a metre cube, because 100 centimetres equals 1 metre.'

   Explain why Nia is wrong.

   b) Work out the dimensions of three different cuboids that have a volume of 100 cm³.

   c) Alec has a set of cubes, all with a side length of 2 centimetres. He needs to fit as many of these cubes as possible into a larger cube with a side length of 10 centimetres.

   How many of the smaller cubes will fit into the larger cube?

   Explain your reasoning.

Maths mastery

Chunky chocolate cubes

Champion chocolate makers, Chunk Choc Co, have developed a brand new chocolate product called Chunky Chocolate Cube.

This special chocolate treat is a cube shape.
It is made of:

- an 'inside' layer of white chocolate
- a 'middle' layer of dark chocolate
- an 'outside' layer of milk chocolate.

Each layer of chocolate is 1 cm thick.
Each cm^3 of chocolate weighs 4 g.

- What is the overall volume of the chocolate in the cube?
- What is the total weight of the Chunky Chocolate Cube?

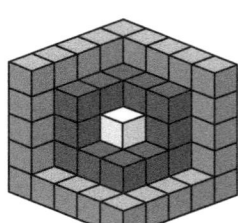

Show the method you used to solve the problem. Is it similar to or different from those used by your classmates?

Support notes

The children have to calculate the volume of a cube that is made up of multiple layers of chocolate. Volume is defined as the amount of space that a 3-D object occupies; take great care not to confuse capacity (the amount something can hold) and volume.

The children will benefit by using cubes to explore this problem. Using different coloured cubes for each layer of chocolate, children can recreate the design of the chocolate cube. They can then count the total number of cubes that they have used. Ask them to record the number of cubes in each layer and the volume of each layer and look for patterns in the results. Extend by asking: *If each layer was 2 cm thick would there be twice as much chocolate?*

Problem solving

Reasoning skills
- Conjecturing and convincing
- Solving problems
- Making comparisons
- Using numerical reasoning

Takeaway trays

A Chinese takeaway has come up with a solution to make its food cheaper – it gets its customers to make their own containers! It provides the paper and the customers make a tray with the largest volume to fit in as much chow mein as possible!

Step 1: Take a 10 cm × 10 cm square.

Step 2: Cut one square from each corner to make a net.

Step 3: Fold the sides to form an open tray.

Step 4: Think about the length, width and height of your tray. What is its volume?

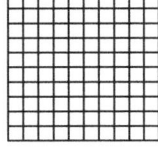
1
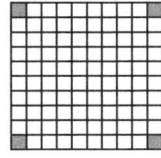
2
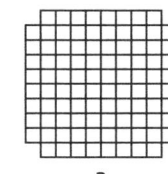
3
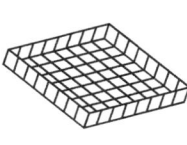
4

Your challenge

First, investigate making different trays using the same square.
What are the different volumes of the trays you make? Which tray has the largest volume?

Things to think about
- Can you define the word 'volume'?
- What shape is a tray?
- How would you find its volume?
- Do you think a wider shorter tray or a narrower taller tray will have a greater volume?
- **What is the link** between the length, width and height of a tray and its volume?
- **Convince me** that you do not need to actually make each tray to work out its volume.
- **What is the same? What is different** about your results?
- Is it **always, sometimes or never true** that a tray's volume increases until it reaches the maximum and then decreases?

75

Tips for success

Children investigate making a tray from a given piece of paper with the greatest possible volume. They then investigate the largest volume they can make from a piece of A4 centimetre-squared paper (whole squares only).

Children will practise using vocabulary such as volume, length, width, height, cuboid, centimetres cubed, measure, taller/shorter, wider/narrower.

The volume of a cube or cuboid is found by multiplying its length by its width by its height. There is flexibility in the side lengths of a cuboid; this investigation explores what happens when, for example, the length decreases but the height increases. Initially, provide children with a 10 cm × 10 cm square of paper to explore what happens when they cut increasingly large squares from all four corners. Their set of results should look like those in the table.

Length (cm)	Width (cm)	Height (cm)	Volume (cm^3)
8	8	1	64
6	6	2	72
4	4	3	48
2	2	4	16

Children can only make cuboids with even lengths and widths. This is because they began with even lengths/widths (10 × 10) and have taken two squares away at a time. To explore odd numbers they would need to begin with odd lengths/widths.

Try this

Support

Provide children with centimetre cubes with which to fill their trays and find their volume. Encourage children to work in pairs and share their results as counting cubes is more time-intensive than using the formula to calculate the volume.

Extension

Divide children into pairs and pose this question: *You have more paper when you start than when you reach the maximum – why does removing paper increase the volume?*

Progress notes

Please use this space to make your own notes.

19 Coordinates and transformations

Thinking starters

1 Use this coordinate grid to plot the points.
   a) Plot the points (4,7), (4,5) and (8,6). Join the points with straight lines, to make a triangle. Reflect the triangle in the x-axis and write the new coordinates of the points.

   b) Plot the points (−4,−2), (−8,−3), (−7,−7) and (−3,−6). Join the points, in order, to make a square. Reflect the square in the y-axis and write down the new coordinates of the points.

   c) Plot the points (5,−2), (2,−6) and (8,−6). Join the points to make a triangle. Reflect the triangle in the x-axis and in the y-axis. Write down the new coordinates of the points.

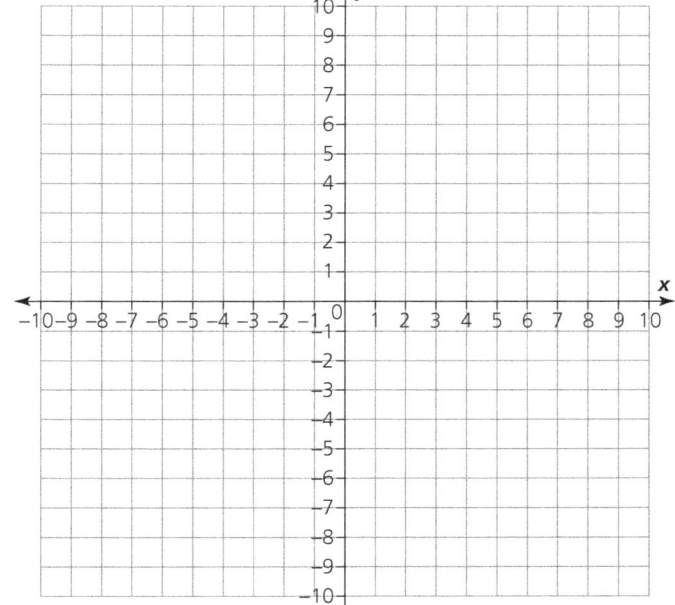

2 Use this coordinate grid to plot the points.
   a) The vertices of a quadrilateral are (−8,−2), (−3,−2), (−9,−4) and (−6,−6). Translate the quadrilateral 6 units right and 8 units up. What are the quadrilateral's new coordinates?

   b) The vertices of a quadrilateral are (−3,3), (2,2), (−1,−1) and (1,−1). Translate the quadrilateral 3 units right and 2 units down. What are the quadrilateral's new coordinates?

   c) Alec plots the vertices of a quadrilateral at the points: (3,−1), (−2,−4), (−1,−5) and (4,−4). He translates the shape 5 units left and 3 units up. He says the new coordinates are (−2,2), (−7,−1), (−7,−3) and (−1,−1).

   Alec makes a mistake with one coordinate. Find Alec's mistake and write the correct coordinate.

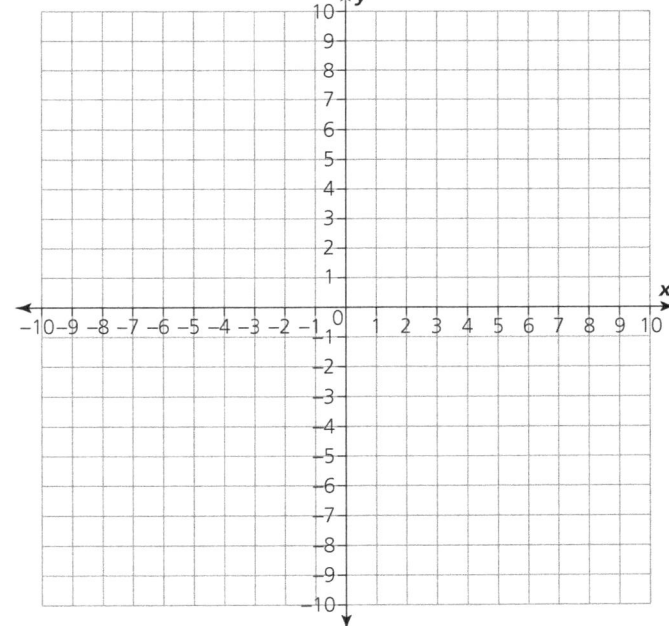

Maths mastery

Translations

Damion draws this triangle on a coordinate grid.

Damion is asked to translate his triangle down 3 and right 5.

- What are the new coordinates of the triangle's vertices?
- Draw the triangle and label its coordinates after the original triangle has been reflected in the y-axis and then translated by two up and six across.

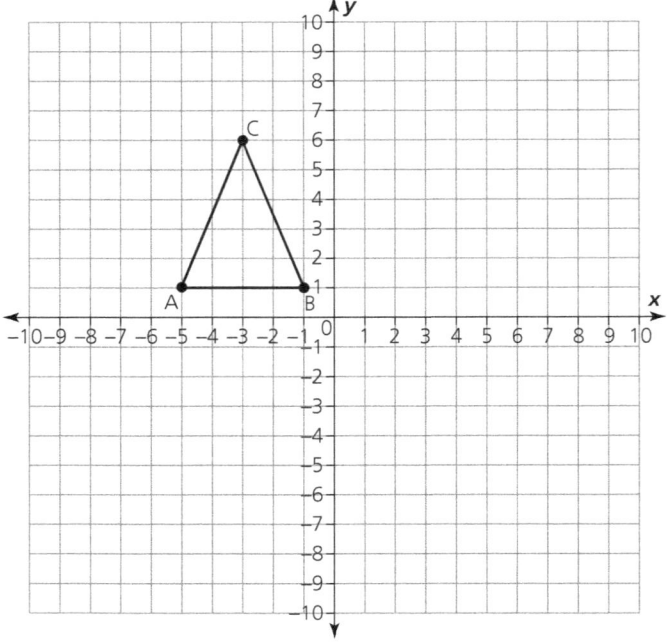

Show the method you used to solve the problem. Is it similar to or different from those used by your classmates?

Support notes

Provide children with a correctly sized triangle and a coordinate grid and encourage them to firstly place it in the original position and then physically move it three squares down and five to the right. Teach ways of remembering the order of coordinates (for example, the phrase 'along the hall, then up the stairs' is a useful way of reminding children that x-axis values should be written first).

Problem solving

Reasoning skills
- Spotting patterns and relationships
- Making connections
- Making generalisations

Crop crosses

Some strange phenomena are appearing in farmers' fields. You may have heard of crop circles, but these are crop crosses! No one knows where they come from.

Each cross is formed by two 'arms' or lines of equal length, crossing over at a central point.

- What are the coordinates for the end of each line?
- Try adding each line's coordinates together. What do you notice?

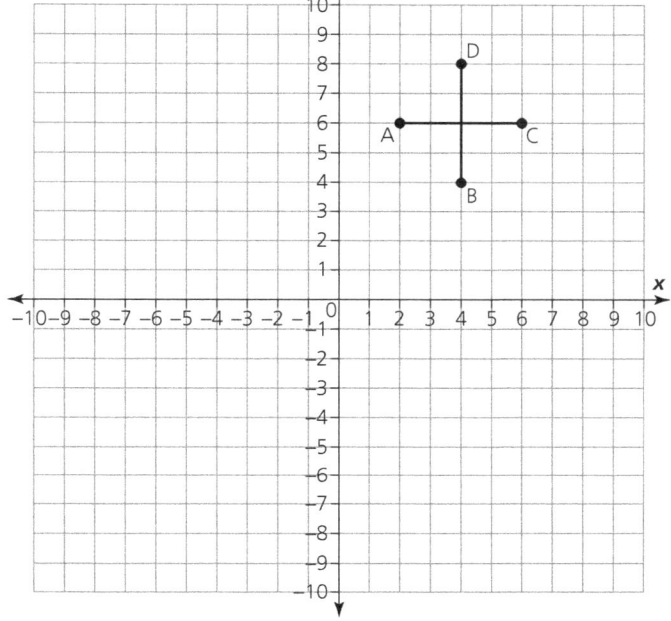

Your challenge

Investigate different sized crosses in different places or at different angles. What do you notice about the coordinates? Can you write a rule for the coordinates? Does the rule always work?

Investigate the coordinates of the middle point in each crop cross. Can you write a rule for finding the middle point every time?

Things to think about
- What do the two numbers in a set of coordinates mean?
- What do the other quadrants in a grid look like?
- What happens when you add a negative and a positive number or two negative numbers?
- **What do you notice** happens when you add the pairs of coordinates that make up the opposite points of a cross? Is this always the case?
- **Convince me** that the rule you have spotted works in any of the four quadrants.
- **What is the link** between the central point of a crop cross and the coordinates of its lines? Can you invent a rule to link them?

79

Tips for success

Children explore the relationship between the coordinates used to form a simple cross shape, using vocabulary such as coordinates, *x*-coordinate, *y*-coordinate, quadrant and terms associated with negative numbers.

The crosses in the investigation are simple + shapes where the 'arms' are equal lengths and cross at a central point. Where each arm is labelled AB and CD, children investigate what happens when they add the coordinates of A and B together and C and D together, for example.

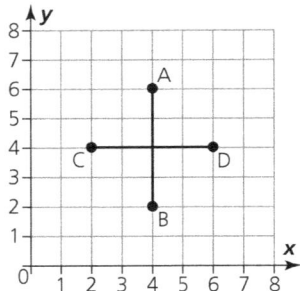

The coordinates for A and B are (4,6) and (4,2) respectively. Added together, this gives (8,8). The coordinates for C and D are (2,4) and (6,4) respectively, also totalling (8,8). This is true of any cross, whatever the size, in all four quadrants and also works for crosses that are at a 45° angle. Children also explore the central point of each cross. The coordinates of this are exactly half the combined coordinates.

Try this

Support
Provide children with a large grid and strips of paper for them to place and make their own crop crosses.

Work within the first quadrant so that children are only adding positive values. Also, limit the type of crosses to vertical so that each middle point is at an intersection of lines.

Extension
Challenge children to make their crop cross more complex (while keeping it symmetrical). For example, they could add diagonal lines. Can they find any links or patterns in the coordinates of their new lines?

Progress notes
Please use this space to make your own notes.

20 Number sequences

Thinking starters

1 Answer these.

   a) Write an expression for the nth term of this sequence.

      4, 10, 16, 22, 28 …

   b) A sequence with the rule '+ 8' begins with 15.

      Will 8888 be in the sequence? Explain your answer.

   c) Aaron writes an 'add 6' sequence beginning at 9.

      Obe writes an 'add 5' sequence beginning at 8.

      What is the first number that will appear in both sequences?

   d) Here are some patterns made from dots.

   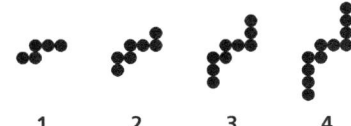

      Write an expression for the nth term of the number sequence for the dots in these patterns. How many dots will there be in the 25th pattern?

   e) Write an expression for the nth term of this sequence.

      8, 11, 14, 17, 20 …

      What number will be the 80th term in the sequence?

2 These black tiles surround an area of white tiles.

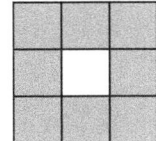 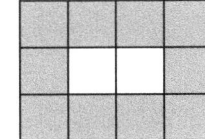 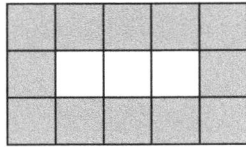

   Draw the next 5 sequences for this pattern.

   If the white tiles are shown as n, work out the formula for the nth term of black tiles.

   Use it to find the 10th term of black tiles.

   Now make up your own pattern and work out what the nth term is.

Maths mastery

Describing sequences

I am making a sequence of T shapes out of squares.

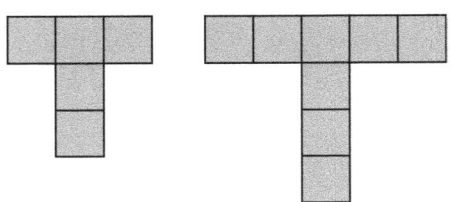

- How many squares will be in each of the next three shapes in my sequence?
- If I have 54 squares, will I be able to make one of these T shapes without having any squares left over?

Show the method you used to solve the problem. Is it similar to or different from those used by your classmates?

Support notes

Use cubes or plastic squares to model each new T shape and encourage children to record their results in a table:

T shape number	Number of squares used
1	5
2	8
3	11
...	...

Children should find it easier to recognise that they are taking three new cubes or squares each time and should be able to translate this into the +3 rule to continue the sequence.

Problem solving

Reasoning skills
- Making generalisations
- Spotting patterns

Pascal's triangle

This is the start of Pascal's triangle.

- Can you work out how Pascal's triangle has been formed?

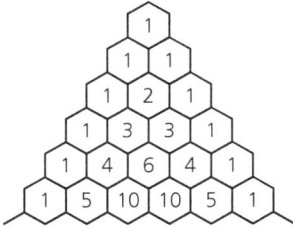

Pascal's triangle is full of patterns; for example, consecutive numbers (1, 2, 3, 4, 5 …).

- What other patterns are there?

Your challenge

Investigate how Pascal's triangle has been created and what patterns exist within the triangle.

Things to think about
- How is the triangle formed? Can you extend it by adding in the next two rows?
- What do you notice about the different diagonals in the triangle?
- If you were to add up any number in any length of the diagonal, where would you find the total of these in the triangle?
- **What do you notice** about numbers in this row/diagonal?
- **What do you notice** about the total of the numbers in each row?
- Is it **always, sometimes, or never** true that each number in the triangle is related to the numbers above it?

Show the method you used to solve the problem. Is it similar to or different from those used by your classmates?

Tips for success

This activity is based on Pascal's triangle. This is a basic version of Pascal's triangle, with six rows (although Pascal numbered row 1 and row 0) and challenges children to extend this and begin to make generalisations.

Pascal's triangle is essentially formed by adding together the two numbers above to make the number below; for example, 15 + 20 = 35. Many patterns can be spotted, which will help with the completion of a larger triangle, including:

- the triangle is symmetrical – this is because it is created from one starting point: 1
- consecutive numbers, for example 1, 2, 3, 4, 5, 6
- triangular numbers, for example 1, 3, 6, 10, 15, 21 – triangular numbers count the objects that could form an equilateral triangle
- the sum of each row doubles; for example, the sum of row 1 is 1, row 2 is 2, row 3 is 4, row 4 is 8, row 5 is 16. The sum of each row is also the consecutive powers of 2, for example 2^1 2^2 2^3 $(2 \times 2 \times 2)$ 2^4 $(2 \times 2 \times 2 \times 2)$ 2^5 and so on.

Try this

Support
The children can access this activity on a level that is appropriate to them. Working in mixed ability groups should provide good opportunity for peer scaffolding of pattern spotting and making generalisations.

Extension
The children should be encouraged to explore less obvious patterns (for example, powers of 2) and begin to try to explain the reasons for the patterns in the triangle.

Progress notes

Please use this space to make your own notes.

21 Finding all possibilities

Thinking starters

1 Gus has three number cards.
   He uses them to make numbers.

   a) How many two-digit numbers can Gus make?

   b) How many three-digit numbers can Gus make?

2 Answer these.

   a) Joshua has four T-shirts and four pairs of shorts. How many combinations of T-shirts and shorts are there?

   b) Joshua buys another T-shirt. How many combinations does he have now?

3 Nia rolls two 1–6 dice and adds the numbers. How many different totals can she make?

4 Answer these.

   a) $3a + b = 15$
      a and b are positive whole numbers. What could a and b be?

   b) $4c - d = 10$
      c and d are positive whole numbers. What could c and d be?

5 Small cans of drink cost 75 cents and large cans cost $1.25. Alec spends $11.25 on cans of drink. How many of each size could Alec have bought?

Maths mastery

Rules for finding unknown numbers

Fatima and Grant are playing a game of guess my numbers.

Fatima says: 'I'm thinking of two numbers. They have a sum of 16 and a product that is an odd number.'

Grant says that there is more than one possible answer.

What are the possible numbers that I could be thinking of?

Show the method you used to solve the problem. Is it similar to or different from those used by your classmates?

Support notes
Encourage children to use number cards and work systematically to make all the pairs that have a sum of 16. They then go through each pair to find those with odd products.

Problem solving

Reasoning skills
- Working systematically
- Finding all possibilities
- Spotting patterns and relationships

The bus stop dilemma

Have you heard the saying about buses? You wait ages for one and then two turn up all at once!

Four people are waiting for the bus. After a long wait, two buses arrive at once and the four people have to choose which bus they get on. They split themselves so that some get on the first bus and some get on the second.

- What are the different ways that they could split themselves?

Your challenge

Investigate the different ways that four people can split themselves between the two buses. What do you notice?

Can you predict the number of ways 100 people might split themselves?

Or an unknown number n?

Invent your own bus stop challenge to investigate. Can you spot any patterns in your results?

Things to think about
- You could use number bonds to help you. What other properties of number could you use?
- How could you use the letter n to explain how to find the number of possible splits?
- How would you make the activity more challenging?
- Give me an example of how five people could split themselves. **Another, another, another**.
- **What is the link** between the number of people and the number of possible splits?
- **Convince me** that you can predict the number of splits, whatever the number of people.
- Give me an example of a way you could extend the challenge and investigate different queues.
- What patterns can you find in your results?

Tips for success

Children explore how a number can be split into different groups. They find patterns in their answers and represent these relationships using algebra.

Initially the problem seems simple, that is, a group of 10 people can be split twice in nine different ways: 9 + 1, 8 + 2, 7 + 3, 6 + 4, 5 + 5, 4 + 6, 3 + 7, 2 + 8 and 1 + 9. Children should generate $n - 1$ to represent this.

The numbers become more interesting when children record only unique splits (for example, 6 + 4 is the same as 4 + 6 so only needs to be recorded once). A group of 10 now only has five possibilities (9 + 1, 8 + 2, 7 + 3, 6 + 4 and 5 + 5). Children should record their results in a table to help find a pattern.

Children may recognise a visual pattern (the numbers go up 5, 5 then 6, 6 then 7, 7). Others may note that the answers are half of the even numbers and might suggest $n \div 2$ to represent this. Children might notice that the odd numbers have the same relationship but are rounded down. Others might consider that, with an odd number, half of the previous number is found instead $((n - 1) \div 2)$.

Try this

Support

Provide children with chains of interlocking cubes. How many different breaks can they make for different chains of cubes? Children can photograph their results or record them by drawing around the splits they make. Let them express rules in words rather than using algebra.

Extension

Ask children to come up with a sequence of images showing how a group grows. Give them the formula $2a$ (where a is the number in the sequence). Ask them to design their sequence to fit this rule. Extend to a more difficult formula if appropriate. A group that grows using the rule $3a + 2$ might look like this:

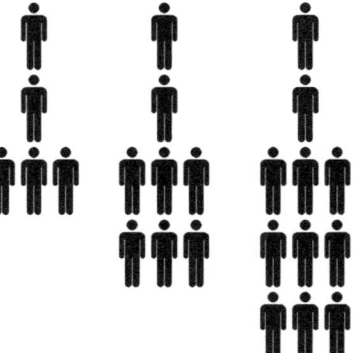

Progress notes

Please use this space to make your own notes.

22 Exploring shapes

Thinking starters

1 Name these 2-D shapes and state three properties of each one.

a) b) c)

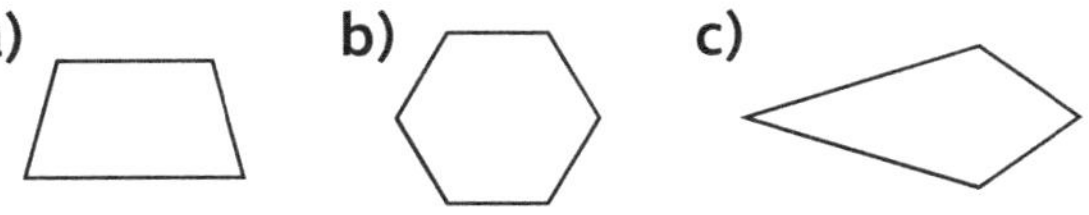

2 My 2-D shape has four equal sides, its opposite sides are parallel, its opposite angles are equal and its diagonals are perpendicular. What shape is it?

3 These are the names of some 2-D shapes.
   A regular hexagon   B square   C equilateral triangle
   D kite   E isosceles triangle   F parallelogram

   Write the letter(s) for the shapes that have these properties:

   a) Has 4 sides:

   b) Has parallel sides:

   c) Has at least 1 line of symmetry:

   d) Its diagonals bisect each other:

   e) Could have at least 1 right angle:

4 Ali has drawn a triangle. He says, 'I measured the angles carefully. The largest angle is three times the smallest angle. The other angle is twice the size of the smallest angle.'
  Work out the sizes of the three angles.

5 Aaron draws a quadrilateral. He says, 'My shape has three right angles but is not a square or a rectangle.'
  What is Aaron's shape? Explain your reasoning.

Maths mastery

Sorting and classifying shapes

Look at the shapes below.

- Sort them into the Carroll diagram by writing the shape letters in the correct section of the diagram.

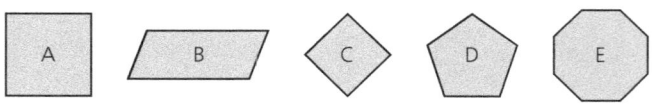

	Perpendicular lines	No perpendicular lines
Pairs of parallel sides		
No pairs of parallel sides		

Show the method you used to solve the problem. Is it similar to or different from those used by your classmates?

Support notes

Go through the process for sorting on a Carroll diagram. Compare it to a Venn diagram if the children are more familiar with those.

Provide children with lots of examples of simple pairs of parallel and perpendicular lines (including those where the two lines are different lengths or thicknesses), before identifying these properties in 2-D shapes.

Provide plastic 2-D shapes for children to physically explore and investigate their properties before sorting.

Problem solving

Reasoning skills
- Working systematically
- Spotting patterns and relationships
- Using algebraic reasoning

Towers of triangles

Look at this triangle. What do you notice about it?

What happens when it is flipped?

By repeating the same triangle and flipping it, we can make an equilateral triangle.

We can then combine lots of triangles to make a tower of triangles.

This tower has 2 rows.

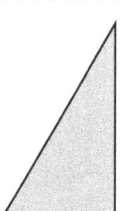

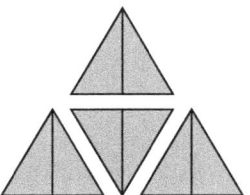

It is made of 4 equilateral triangles and 8 right-angled triangles. It contains 1 downward-pointing triangle and 3 upward-pointing triangles.

Your challenge

Explore what happens when more rows are added to the tower of triangles. Look at the different numbers of triangles used. Can you find any patterns?

If there are 100 rows, can you predict any of the numbers?

What about n rows, can you write any rules to help?

Things to think about
- What is an equilateral triangle? What is a right-angled triangle?
- What does the right-angled triangle need to make it an equilateral triangle when it is flipped?
- What sort of information can we record about our towers?
- Give me a number of triangles that might make a tower. **Another, another, another**.
- **What is the link** between the row number and the number of small triangles you need to use to make it?
- **What do you notice** about the number of downward-pointing triangles and the number of upward-pointing triangles in each tower?
- If we are looking at the 10th row of a tower of triangles, **what else do we know?**

Tips for success

Children build towers of triangles, made by flipping right-angled triangles in different ways to form a pattern of equilateral triangles. There are many different patterns they can explore as a result.

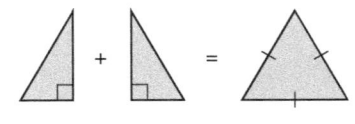

The right-angled triangles used in this investigation are those that form an equilateral triangle when flipped and placed side by side.

The 'towers of triangles' in this investigation are made by placing these equilateral triangles in rows, some pointing upwards and some pointing downwards.

The numbers that result are interesting. Children should record their results in table form and then look for and explain the different patterns they see.

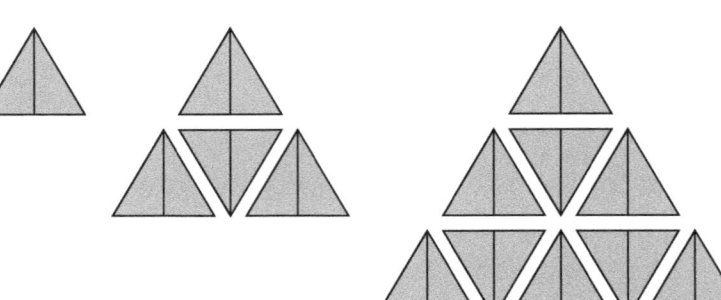

Once children notice patterns in their answers, they should explore these types of numbers further, write formulae and use them to predict much larger towers of triangles.

Try this

Support

Initially, give children equilateral triangles and encourage them to explore the numbers involved in making towers of triangles. These will be square numbers. Encourage children to take each number of cubes and use them to form squares to check.

Extension

Discuss the link between the upward pointing equilateral triangles (triangular numbers), the downward pointing ones (triangular numbers) and the total number (square numbers).

The first two added together make the third, so two triangular numbers added together make a square number. Challenge children to write the square numbers to 100 and make each by adding two triangular numbers. Does it work for every square number? Is there only one way?

Progress notes

Please use this space to make your own notes.

23 Money problems

Thinking starters

1 The Allen family has saved $985 towards their summer holiday. The cost of the holiday is $3019. How much more do they need to save?

2 These are the food and drink choices at a cinema.

Large popcorn	Small popcorn	Drink	Hot dog	Ice cream
$3.10	$2.75	$1.85	$4.15	$2.50

Malik buys a large box of popcorn, a drink and an ice cream.
Andre buys a small popcorn, a drink and hot dog.
Who spends more money?

3 Ali bought 3 CDs for $15.99 each. His brother bought another 2 CDs at $13.99 each. How much did they spend altogether?

4 Each week Kim saves half of her pocket money for a DVD player. It takes her 30 weeks to save the $75 she needs. How much is her pocket money per week?

5 A computer is priced at $450 in Bargain Buys. The same computer costs $550 in Budget Bytes, but then the price is reduced by 20% in a sale. In which shop is the computer cheaper? By how much?

6 A second-hand shop has two offers.
   5 computer games for $25   8 computer games for $35
   Nisha and Tia buy some games. Nisha says, 'I bought more games than Tia for less money.'
   Show how this is possible.

Maths mastery

Food shopping

Each week, Saul's mother spends $47 on food shopping.

- How much money does she spend in 4 weeks?
- In half a year, how much money will she spend?

Key fact: remember there are 52 weeks in a year.

Show the method you used to solve the problem. Is it similar to or different from those used by your classmates?

Support notes

Provide ready-drawn 2 × 2 grids to scaffold the use of the grid method. Children can then complete these.

To help with partitioning each number, children can use place-value cards to make each number and then separate them out into their tens and ones.

Place-value counters may also be used to model the numbers using the grid method.

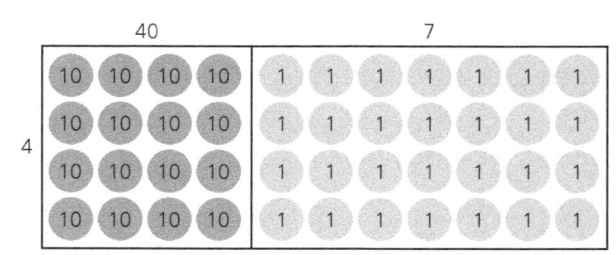

Problem solving

Juice for school

One 750 ml bottle of concentrated orange squash will make twenty-five 240 ml cups of diluted orange squash.

- If you want to give each adult and child in your school a drink of orange squash, how much concentrated orange squash will you need to buy?
- How much water would you use?

250 ml bottle = $110
750 ml bottle = $310
1.5 litre bottle = $550
5 litre bottle = $1640

Things to think about
- How many adults and children are there in your school?
- How much squash is in each glass?
- What is the cheapest way to buy the amount of squash you need? Will you have any squash left over?
- **What do you notice** about the relationship between the bottle of squash and how many cups they make?
- If we know that 750 ml of squash makes twenty-five 240 ml cups, **what else do we know?**

Your challenge

Work out how much squash and water would be needed to make a cup of squash for everyone in the school.

What is the cheapest way of buying squash at these prices?

Show the method you used to solve the problem. Is it similar to or different from those used by your classmates?

95

Tips for success

In this investigation, the children use relationships between different quantities to solve a problem.

Children need to work out how much squash and water is in each cup and therefore how much squash they need to buy.

In the problem, 750 ml of orange squash makes twenty-five 240 ml cups. Therefore, there is 30 ml of squash in each 240 ml cup and so there must also be 210 ml of water in each 240 ml cup.

This reasoning can then be used to work out how much squash is needed to cater for your entire school. The children can then use the price list given to work out the cheapest way to purchase this squash.

In the problem, the ratio of the juice to squash is 30:210, which can be simplified to 1:7.

This can then be used to work out that in a 160 ml cup of juice, you would need 20 ml of juice (8 parts in total, therefore each part is equal to 160 ml divided by 8).

Try this

Support

This problem can easily be re-created practically (although providing enough squash for everyone in school may be a bit too much to re-create!). Initially, ask children to split 750 ml of squash between 25 cups and extend thinking and understanding from this point. For children struggling with the concept of ratio and proportion, different coloured cubes can be used to represent the relative ratios.

Extension

Challenge the children to work out how much squash is needed to make a 160 ml cup of drink for everyone in your school.

Progress notes

Please use this space to make your own notes.

24 Scaling and ratio

Thinking starters

1. A square has a length of 12 cm. Work out the new length if it is resized by a scale factor of:
   a) 6
   b) 1/2
   c) 0.25

2. Answer these.
   a) A rectangle, with a length of 8 cm, is resized. The new length is 40 cm. What scale factor has been used?
   b) The diameter of a circle is 20 cm. It is redrawn with a diameter of 50 cm. What scale factor has been used?
   c) A plan uses a scale of 1 cm:1 m. What scale factor has been used?
   Explain your reasoning.

3. A flagpole is 6 metres tall and casts a shadow 2.4 metres long. A tree beside it casts a shadow 6 metres long. How tall is the tree?
   Explain your reasoning.

4. Samir says, 'There are 30 children. Boys and girls are in the ratio of 5:3 in the class.'
   Explain why Samir is wrong.

5. Toby and Noah share a job. Toby works for 3 hours and Noah works for 2 hours. They are paid $60 and share the pay. Toby gets $45 and Noah gets $15.
   Noah says that this is not fair. Do you agree?
   Explain your answer.

6. Parcel A is three times heavier than Parcel B.
   Parcel B is three times heavier than Parcel C.
   Parcel A weighs 1.8 kg.
   How heavy is Parcel C?

Maths mastery

Scaling problems

Saira wants to have a large version of her favourite photo put onto a canvas, to put on her wall.

A shop offers to print the photo on a canvas that is three times larger than her photo.

Saira's photo is 15 cm wide by 7 cm tall.

- What will the dimensions of Saira's canvas print be?

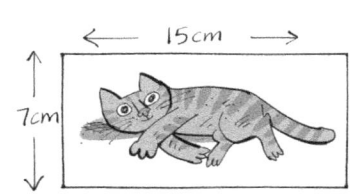

Show the method you used to solve the problem. Is it similar to or different from those used by your classmates?

Support notes

Use pieces of paper placed next to each other to show what happens when a rectangle is enlarged by a scale factor of 2. Move from doubling the dimensions to considering enlargements with different scale factors. Encourage children to build up the ratio in table form as follows:

Scale factor	Width	Height
1	15 cm	7 cm
2	30 cm	14 cm
3	45 cm	21 cm

Problem solving

Reasoning skills
- Conjecturing and convincing
- Solving problems
- Using numerical reasoning

Going crackers!

Jacob's uncle brings maths into everything. When he comes to visit, it is like having tea with your teacher!

At teatime, he says to Jacob, 'You're 10 and I'm 30. So this plate of cream crackers should be split in the same ratio.'

Jacob has to do some thinking …

Your challenge

Explore the different numbers of crackers that Jacob and his uncle can divide in the same ratio as their ages, that is 1:3.

What other totals would mean they have a whole number of crackers?

What if Jacob and his uncle have five crackers between them? How can they split them into the same ratio?

Try this for other numbers of crackers. Can you come up with a rule to help you?

Things to think about
- What is a ratio?
- What is the ratio that Jacob's uncle is talking about?
- How can you investigate the different numbers that can be shared?
- What might be a good way of recording your results?
- Is it **always, sometimes or never true** that a group of crackers split in the ratio 1:3 will make two whole numbers?
- Give me a **hard and an easy** example of something that has been split in the ratio 1:3.
- **What is the link** between division and ratio?

Show the method you used to solve the problem. Is it similar to or different from those used by your classmates?

Tips for success

Children devise a ratio to reflect the different ages of two characters, then explore ways of dividing quantities of cream crackers according to that ratio. In particular, they consider ways of splitting quantities where the resulting groups are not whole numbers.

A ratio is a way of expressing one number or quantity in terms of another; for example, the ratio 1 to 5 (which can also be written 1:5) means that for every 1 of something, there are 5 of something else.

In this investigation, one character is three times as old as the other. The ratio of their ages is 1:3.

As they investigate, children should notice the relationship between multiplication tables and the number of crackers each person has.

Encourage children to explore dividing numbers that are not multiples of 4. These can be split into the same ratio if the remainder is expressed as a fraction (each remaining cracker is cut into quarters, which are shared out 1:3); for example, 5 crackers can be shared out as $1\frac{1}{4}:3\frac{3}{4}$.

Try this

Support
Make the task more practical by providing squares of paper for children to divide physically (for example, 4 crackers to share in the ratio 1:3). Encourage children to add another group, similarly split, and to record the new numbers each person has. Can children identify the links between multiplication table facts and the groups they create each time?

Extension
Children could consider different ratios. For example, if Jacob's father is 40, how might he split 10 crackers with his son? What about 11 or 12 crackers? Jacob's brother is 5. How might Jacob use the same idea to share some crackers?

Progress notes

Please use this space to make your own notes.

25 Division problems

Thinking starters

1 Answer these.

a) Eggs are packed in boxes of 12.
   Work out the fewest number of boxes needed for 1300 eggs.

b) Hakim says, 'One way to divide by 24, is to divide by 3 and then divide by 8.'
   Is Hakim correct? Find alternative ways of dividing by 24.

c) What could the missing numbers be?

   900 ÷ ☐ = ☐ ÷ 30

2 Solve these problems.

a) Aymee eats half a pizza and eats half of what is left the next day. How much of the pizza has Aymee eaten?

b) Which would give the most pieces of pizza: dividing 8 pizzas into fifths or dividing 7 pizzas into sixths?

c) Liam shares 6 pizzas with some friends. Each of them gets $\frac{3}{4}$ of a pizza. How many shared the pizza?

d) Four friends share half of a box of sweets. What fraction of the whole box does each friend get?

e) Ayesha has a jar of small and large counters. One-fifth of the counters are large. There are equal numbers of red, blue and yellow counters. What fraction of the counters are large and red?

3 Riel says, 'If you divide a fraction by a positive whole number, the fraction always gets smaller.'
Is this always, sometimes or never true?

Maths mastery

Dividing fractions

Simone's mom says she can share $\frac{1}{2}$ of a large chocolate cake between her and her four friends.

- What fraction of the whole cake do Simone and her four friends each get?

Show the method you used to solve the problem. Is it similar to or different from those used by your classmates?

Support notes

Check that the children visualise the problem correctly. If they incorrectly answer $\frac{1}{5}$, they may have either found the fraction of the portion (each person gets $\frac{1}{5}$ of the portion) or they are visualising a whole cake split into five rather than $\frac{1}{2}$ a cake split into five. Encourage children to model the problem by drawing a circle on a piece of paper. They could physically cut the circle into half and then fifths to simulate cutting the cake.

Problem solving

Reasoning skills
- Making generalisations
- Spotting patterns

Divisibility

You can tell if any number is divisible by 2, by looking at the last digit and seeing if this is even.

This means that you can see straightaway that 12 872 is divisible by 2, whereas 87 433 is not divisible by 2.

You can also tell if numbers are divisible by 3, 4, 5, 6, 9 or 10. (It is also possible to tell if numbers are divisible by 7 and 8 but that is much trickier to do!)

Your challenge

Write out how you can tell if any number is divisible by 3, 4, 5, 6, 9 or 10.

Don't forget: divisible means when one number can be divided into another, giving a whole number answer.

Things to think about
- How are you going to try to spot the rules?
- How are you going to explain your divisibility tests?
- Can you explain why your divisibility tests work?
- Are some divisibility tests harder to explain than others? Why?
- **What is the same? What is different** between these (multiples of *x*)?
- **Convince me** that this is the divisibility rule for *x*.
- **What do you notice** about numbers that are multiples of *x*?

Show the method you used to solve the problem. Is it similar to or different from those used by your classmates?

Tips for success

The children investigate the divisibility tests for 2, 3, 4, 5, 6, 9 and 10, that is, how we can tell if a number is divisible by these numbers exactly/if a number is a multiple of these numbers. A divisibility test for 7 is excluded as it is tricky to identify and understand. A divisibility test for 8 is a good challenge as an extension.

Some of the divisibility tests rely on the digit sum and digit root of a number. A digit sum is the value achieved when you add up all the digits in a number; for example, digit sum of 98 is 9 + 8 = 17. A digit root is the number achieved when you keep finding the digit sum until you reach a single-digit number; for example, digit sum of 98 is 8: 9 + 8 = 17 and then 1 + 7 = 8.

Here are the rules for the divisibility of 2, 3, 4, 5, 6, 9 and 10:

Divisibility rule for 2: the last digit in the number is even

Divisibility rule for 5: the last digit in the number is a 5 or 0

Divisibility rule for 3: the digit root of the number is a multiple of 3 (so 3, 6 or 9)

Divisibility rule for 4: if the last two digits are a multiple of 4, then the whole number is divisible by 4

Divisibility rule for 6: if a number is divisible by both 2 and 3 it is divisible by 6

Divisibility rule for 9: the digit root of the number is 9

Divisibility rule for 10: the last digit is 0. This is because the first multiple of 10 is 10.

Try this

Support

The children may benefit from using a multiplication square, along with a wider list of numbers that are multiples of the numbers you wish them to investigate.

Extension

The children should be encouraged to begin to try to explain the reasons the divisibility tests work and the connections between the different groups (for example, 3, 6 and 9). When finding the divisibility rule for 8 (the last three digits are a multiple of 8) ask them to relate this to the rules for 2 and 4. They may see the link between 10 (and all multiples of 10) being divisible by 2, 100 (and all multiples of 100) being divisible by 4 and 1000 (and all multiples of 1000) being divisible by 8.

Progress notes

Please use this space to make your own notes.

26 Circles and shapes

Thinking starters

1. On this centimetre-squared paper, draw:

   a) a pentagon with three right angles.

   b) a parallelogram with a length of 7 cm and a height of 4 cm.

   c) a trapezium with two right angles and parallel sides measuring 6 cm and 3 cm.

2. Answer these.

   a) Explain the word 'circumference'.

   b) Explain the word 'radius'.

   c) The diameter of a circle is 27 cm. What is the length of its radius?

3. Complete the table.

   Fill in the first 2 columns using the rule $d = 2r$.

   Now complete the rest of the table when the circles are increased by a scale factor of 3.

Radius	Diameter	Increase by a scale factor of 3	
		New radius	New diameter
9 cm			
4 m			
	24 cm		
7.5 cm			
	1 m		

Maths mastery

Circles

Monique has a circular paper plate. She has been asked to label the radius, diameter and circumference.

- Can you help her by labelling the radius, diameter and circumference on the circle below?

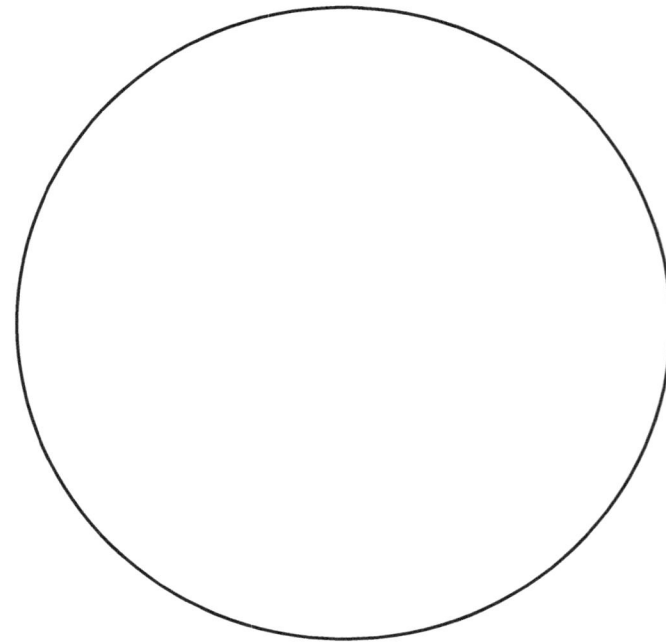

- Complete this sentence to show the relationship between the radius and the diameter:

The radius is _____ the diameter.

Support notes

Provide children with paper circles to fold in order to show the radius and circumference. Encourage them to cut lengths of string the length of the radius and diameter and to compare them (this can be a clearer way of identifying that the radius is twice the length of the diameter).

Children should be able to relate radius, diameter and circumference to everyday instances.

Ask: *Jayden has a bicycle. Each wheel has metal spokes that go from the centre of the wheel to the outside. Is each spoke the length of the radius, diameter or circumference of the circle?*

Ask: *How could Jayden show the diameter of a circle using his wheel?* (It is the distance from one side of the wheel to the other, going through the middle of the wheel.)

Ask: *Jayden draws a chalk mark on the floor and then pushes his bike so that the wheel goes around once. He then draws another chalk mark to show the distance. Is this the same as the radius, the diameter or the circumference of the circle?* (The circumference) *Why?* (It is the distance around a circle and so it is the mastery the wheel travels if it goes around once.)

Problem solving

Reasoning skills
- Working systematically
- Finding all possibilities
- Making generalisations

Four-sided force fields

A spaceship is encircled by 8 enemy alien craft!

They are equally spaced and preparing to attack.

The aliens fire 4 lasers from one craft to another to trap the spaceship, surrounding it with a force field.

This is one of the shapes they make.

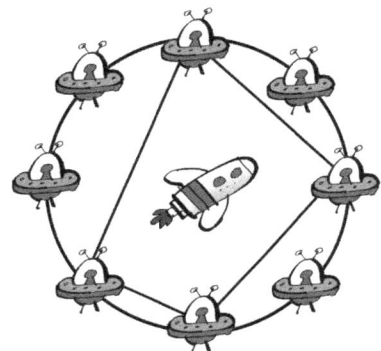

The only possible way for the spaceship to escape is to predict the different shapes the aliens will make.

Your challenge
Help the spaceship crew by investigating how many different shapes the aliens can make with their four-sided force field.

Things to think about
- What is the name for any four-sided shape?
- How many names of four-sided shapes do you know?
- How would you recognise one of these shapes if you saw one? (Think about the lengths of the sides and the angle sizes.)
- Is there a way to make sure you find different shapes and don't repeat any?
- **What is the same? What is different** about a kite and a rectangle?
- A kite, a rectangle, a square and a trapezium. **Which is the odd one out?**
- Is it **always, sometimes or never true** that a quadrilateral has four corners?
- **Convince me** that all the shapes you have found are different.

Show the method you used to solve the problem. Is it similar to or different from those used by your classmates?

107

Tips for success

Children investigate all the possible four-sided shapes they can make by joining four dots from a set of eight, equally spaced around a circle.

This activity will help children to practise the language of geometry, such as quadrilateral, square, rectangle, trapezium and kite. Encourage children to describe properties of 2-D shapes using terms like sides, vertices and angles as well as equal, parallel, 90°, and so on.

The various shapes children may discover are:

- square (all sides the same length, 90° angles, a special kind of regular rectangle)
- rectangle (opposite sides the same length, 90° angles)
- trapezium (one pair of opposite sides is parallel)
- kite (two pairs of sides equal, diagonals cross at 90°).

Children will discover a square rotated 45° and many will name this a diamond. This is a common misconception. Explore this with children by rotating their piece of paper 45° and asking the name of the shape now. Does the type of shape change when the paper is turned?

Try this

Support
Give children a pegboard to manipulate the shapes as they explore them. Give the same alien force-field scenario, but remove the limitation of the circle split into eight. Ask children to make as many different four-sided force fields as they can. They make different shapes on the same pegboard so they can compare each shape visually. Talk about the shapes they know and what makes them that shape.

Extension
Encourage children to consider the area of the shapes they have drawn. Which shape has the smallest/largest area? Is there any way to find out for sure?

Ask: *What if there were five laser beams? How many different shapes could you make? Would the number of shapes change if there were more than eight alien craft?*

Progress notes

Please use this space to make your own notes.

27 Angles

Thinking starters

1 Calculate the unknown angles.

a)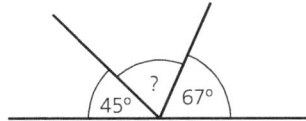

b)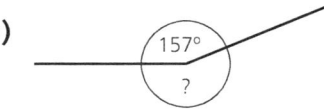

c)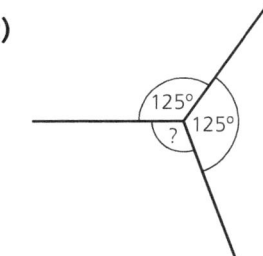

d)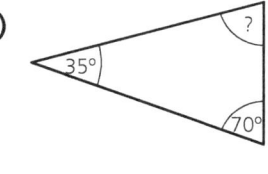

e)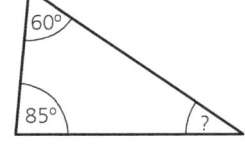

2 Five lines meet at a point, forming equal angles. What is the size of each angle?

3 An elastic band has been put around some of the pins on this pinboard.

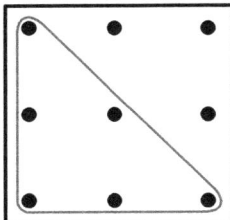

What are the sizes of the three angles formed?
Explain how you know.

4 Alec draws a rectangle with its diagonals, as shown. He measures one angle of 65°.

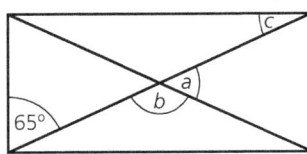

Calculate the angles labelled a, b and c. Show your working, explaining each step.

5 In a parallelogram, one angle is 35°. What are the other three angles?
Explain your answer.

Maths mastery

Missing angle problems

Designers often sketch their drawings to work out the angles.

- Can you help the designers by filling in the missing angles?

a)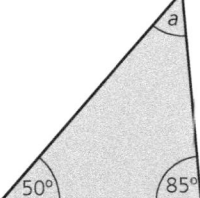

b)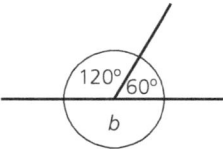

c)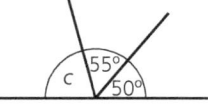

d)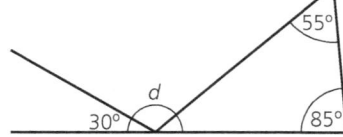

Show the method you used to solve the problem. Is it similar to or different from those used by your classmates?

Support notes

Use paper to physically demonstrate the facts about angles. If children know that the corner of a piece of paper is 90°, they can see that two corners next to each other make a straight line and 90 + 90 = 180°. Four corners will go all the way around and 90 × 4 = 360°. Similarly, if they cut out any triangle, rip each corner off and place them side by side, the angles will always make a straight line (so they must total 180°). Teach children the *What do I know? How can I use it to help?* concept to use these facts to help answer each question.

Problem solving

Reasoning skills
- Making conjectures
- Spotting patterns
- Making connections

Kieron's crazy angles

Kieron draws two lines that cross over each other, like this:

Then he draws another two like this:

Kieron measures each angle he has created, in both drawings. He then looks for patterns ... but he would like your help!

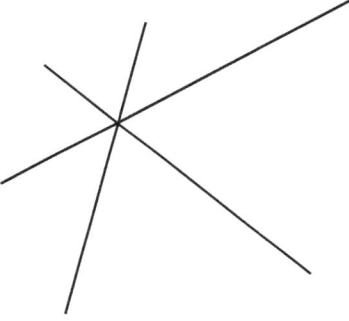

Your challenge

Investigate what you notice about the four angles created when two lines cross over.

How is it the same and how is it different when three lines cross over?

Things to think about
- What do you notice about the sizes of the angles?
- What do you notice about the sum of all the angles?
- Are any of the angles the same size? Is this **always, sometimes or never true**?
- Is it **always, sometimes or never true** that angles at a point add to 360°?
- **What is the same? What is different** between these sets of lines?
- If we know the value of two angles, **what else do we know**?
- **What is the link** between angles that are opposite each other?

Tips for success

Children investigate the relationships between angles formed by two, and then three, lines that cross at a central point. The point at which the lines intersect is called a 'vertex'.

Ask them to discuss, in pairs, what they notice about the relationship between the angles (without measuring). Share some ideas as a class and record them on an 'Our conjectures' board. Encourage children to use the term 'conjecture', a mathematical term that they should be familiar with; it means thoughts or theory. Encourage them to realise that their conjectures can keep changing and evolving as they discover more information and try more examples.

When measuring the values of the angles, children should notice that all the angles around a point total 360°, regardless of the number of angles at the point. They should also notice that the angles opposite each other have the same value.

Pairs of opposite angles that meet at a vertex are called 'vertically opposite angles' (note that vertically in this instance refers to the angles sharing the same vertex, not the usual meaning of up/down).

Children should also notice that each pair, or trio, of angles formed by each straight line add to 180°. This is because all angles on a straight line add up to 180°. Any angles that are on one straight line, and therefore add up to 180°, are called 'supplementary angles'.

Children may struggle initially with making accurate measurements using a protractor. Revise the use of a protractor with the class or individual groups if necessary. Ensure children read from the correct scale when reading the angle.

Try this

Support
If children struggle with measuring four angles, they could begin by investigating patterns in the two angles around a point made on a line before progressing to the main problem.

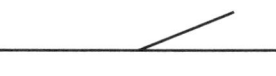

Extension
Ask children to discuss and make conjectures about a different kind of drawing, for example:

Does the conjectures list they made earlier help them to make further conjectures about this drawing?

Progress notes

Please use this space to make your own notes.